Date Due

Hogg, the Seven Last Words

Barry Callaghan

McArthur & Company
Toronto

Published in Canada by McArthur & Company, 2001
322 King Street West, Suite 402
Toronto, ON, M5V 1J2

National Library of Canada Cataloguing in Publication Data

Callaghan, Barry, 1937 –
  Hogg, the seven last words

Poems
ISBN 1-55278-246-8

        I.   Title.

PS8555.A49H628 2001   C811'.54   C2001-901633-6
PR9199.3.C35H628 2001

Earlier versions of some of these poems appeared in *As Close As We Came*.
Three poems, Tricksters, Promise of Rain, and Osip Mandelstam Moves His Lips,
appeared in *Grain*.

ACKNOWLEDGEMENT
  All Around the World (Turner) © 1993 Rhino Records Inc.
  10635 Santa Monica Blvd., Los Angeles, CA 90025-4900
  *Every reasonable effort has been made to find ownership of copyrighted material. Any information
  enabling the publisher to rectify any right or credit in future printings will be welcomed.*

Composition and Design by *Michael P. Callaghan*
Typeset at *Moons of Jupiter, Inc*
Cover by *Mad Dog Design Connection, Inc.*
Author Photo by *Ingrid Scherer-Mohr*
Printed and Bound in Canada by *Transcontinental Printing, Inc.*

The publisher wishes to acknowledge the financial support of the Government of
Canada through the Book Publishing Industry Development Program (BPIDP)
and the Canada Council for our publishing activities. The publisher further wishes
to acknowledge the financial support of the Ontario Arts Council for our pub-
lishing program.

10 9 8 7 6 5 4 3 2 1

for
Claire, my Crazy Jane

Contents

Not a Thorn, Not a Tree · 1

Air, Air, Air · 2

At the Station of the Noseless Slut · 4

Ice Fishing · 5

He Loved a Floating Apple · 6

To Turn Again · 7

Sour Grapes · 8

Stones · 9

Café Society · 10

Himmler's Law · 11

Cold Comfort · 13

Sun Dance · 14

The Astoria Hotel · 15

The Maiming · 16

As Times Goes By · 17

Ambush · 18

Sleepwalker · 19

A Stolen Kiss · 20

Fire and Water · 21

Letters · 22

The Glass Heart · 23

A Gaunt Note · 25

Promise of Rain · 26

Osip Mandelstam Moves His Lips · 29

Moving · 30

All Ears · 31

x, the Starting Number · 32

A Doll's Nest · 33

The Jubjub Bird · *34*

Hogg Attends a Performance of *The Exile* at
   Café Tristan Bernard · *35*

Snowflake · *36*

Hogg Meets Isaac Babel · *37*

The Old Believer · *38*

Great Peter · *39*

Hogg Goes to the Movies · *40*

Amputated Love · *41*

Khishchuk and Ugolov, 1984: A Legal Fragment · *42*

The Wound · *43*

So It Is Said · *44*

Champagne · *46*

Heartbeat · *47*

Foundling · *48*

Cradle Song · *49*

Christa: A Miracle · *50*

Bluebeard · *51*

Rasputin · *52*

Lovesick · *54*

What Voznesensky Whispered to Hogg · *55*

WANTED: A POPOV MACHINE · *56*

A Mute Chord · *57*

Wishboned · *58*

Mon Grand Guignol · *59*

At the Beach · *61*

The White Fairy Tale · *62*

Sky Queen · *63*

Tell It Slant · *64*

Hogg in the Land of H. · *65*

A Blown Kiss · *66*

Her Mother · *67*

Stasis · *68*

Orphans · *69*

Homesick · *71*

At the Winter Palace · *72*

A Little Piece of the Night · *74*

Fathers & Sons · *76*

On Nevsky Prospekt · *77*

Hunger · *79*

An Evening Drive · *80*

The Eyes Have It · *81*

The Note · *82*

Passports · *83*

Tear · *85*

All Found · *86*

A Cold Child · *87*

Trumps · *88*

A Bird Peeped · *90*

Tricksters · *91*

How Would You Feel · *92*

Home Fires · *93*

Stigmata · *94*

The Acrobat · *96*

Hogg on 96 Point 6 · *97*

Hogg All Found · *98*

Hogg Is Accosted by a Former Dance Instructor Now
   One-legged Who Is Moonlighting as a Juggler · *99*

Phoenix · *100*

The Golden Egg · *102*

Bruegel's Two Monkeys · *103*

In a Minor Key · *104*

On the Dong Beat · *105*

There Is No Lenin But Lenin · *106*

Inside Out · *107*

Tomorrow's Man · *108*

The Dog Days of History · *110*

At Dostoievsky's Grave · *111*

Shearing · *112*

Hogg Speaks of Simple Mathematics · *113*

Hogg Attends a Café Performance
   of Appollinaire's *The Poet Assassinated* · *114*

The Leningrad Evening News · *115*

Her Potato Song · *117*

Escape Route · *118*

The Grinder · *119*

Then There Were Eleven · *120*

Bird Song · *121*

Smerdikov's Fish Song · *122*

Puppy Love · *123*

As Close as They Came · *124*

True Love · *125*

So It Was Done · *126*

Canto XXXIV · *127*

Seven Last Words · *128*

Hope · *129*

Hogg's Notes · *131*

Acknowledgement · *153*

Books by Barry Callaghan · *154*

L'Invitation au voyage

Mon enfant, ma soeur,
Songe à la douceur
D'aller là-bas vivre ensemble!
Aimer à loisir,
Aimer et mourir
Au pays qui te ressemble!
Les soleils mouillés
De ces ciels brouillés
Pour mon esprit ont les charmes
Si mystérieux
De tes traîtres yeux,
Brilliant à travers leurs larmes.

— CHARLES BAUDELAIRE

Hogg, the Seven Last Words

Not a Thorn, Not a Tree

Like the seed
of
an unborn
bird
in
its egg,
he waited
to
feather
his wings
and
sing:

Footloose, a knee.
It's only a knee, no more.
Not a thorn, not a tree.
Just a knee, no more.

A soldier knee-deep
in blood bled to death.
A bone of breath-
less guile, a knee,

went to explore for a while
the world, a knee,
not a thorn, not a tree,
only a knee, no more.

Air, Air, Air

Sleepwalking
in Noah's muddy shoes, Hogg was
staggered by Ham and Shem
who cooked

the knucklebones
of all the animals over kindling cut
from the ark and warned him he was next.
The worms he heard

cuckooing were a kind
of wooing undying as the gravedigger's
pace on the heels of men who'd disappeared
without a trace.

Curiosity plus dread was his curse.
He sped due west with the dove to Dachau
where he pinned the bird's agog eye
to the oven's bridal bed,

bread so burned to ash
he tore his prayers out
by the hair and cried, O god,
this is the awfullest

ever hour of lead. The bird said,
Standing aghast in a pocket
of unknowing is no excuse: eating your own
goes back to before

the begats. Love is
a caveat. Hogg limped on alone to Leningrad, Number 7
Pergevalsky, sat down to tea spiked
with homebrewed alcohol

in Raskolnikov's yellow room
where Dostoievsky, playing double solitaire
with the pawnbroker for the axe, cocked
an eye and said,

All light seeds the dark,
total darkness is irretrievable and so too
despair. All men need is
air, air, air.

At the Station of the Noseless Slut

He swallowed
guile,
fear and bile

and
crawled
into the echo

of
blood
in an hourglass

where the words
he heard
stood on their heads,

font, door, bride,
the gun,
the dying scream

astride
the laugh
that would be

his
epitaph,
and later,

perhaps
a
rose.

Ice Fishing

He saw
ice inlaid in light
along the canal

and old men
fishing
for their sons

under birch trees
hung
with the severed tongues

of bells tolled
at
Lubyanka

where bodies were laid out
pearled with blood
beside

skinning bowls
made from the silver spoons
of those

who died
looking for air
holes

in the ice
filled with the blue
sky and hooks.

He Loved a Floating Apple

He loved a floating apple in the night.
Treeless, twigless,
he loved a floating apple tree in the night,
rootless, branches weighing down the night.

And the whole earth, afloat in the night,
not tethered to anyone.
He loved darkness that didn't disappear
as he woke again

but kept a distance, unseen
and then, as the sun set, drew near.
He saw someone approaching,
emerging from the dark, merging into dark again.

To Turn Again

Her
eyes
as dark
as
a
starless
night
were
stars
that led
him
in to
the
light.

Sour Grapes

In Saint Isaak's Square
facing the Astoria hotel
two dead men were talking
about what it was like
to listen in on life.
"It's never over."
Their laughter became the wet green grapes
dipped in salt broken open
between her teeth
to a sweetness she passed into
Hogg's mouth with a kiss. And then
came the salt: "Two pieces of advice—
assume you are being watched and wiretapped,
and trust no one offering to be your friend."
"Thank you," he said,
and she, freeing a seed
from between her teeth with her tongue said,
"You just made your first mistake."

Stones

She came to him at the canal casting flowers
into an odor of wet leather under the Fontanka bridge.
Launching a small boat in the acetylene light
they set out looking for her father on the floor of the lagoon.
An aloof, leery man, she said, who kept mourning doves,
but one day unlocked his cage
on the roof, scowled at the birds
who refused to fly away and went out on the water.
"They dragged for a week.
Maybe he went up instead of down."
She crossed the salt air with a ribbon from her undone hair,
lifted the lipstick mirror from her purse
and wore it like a monocle to make him laugh.
On the far shore the clockface in the spire had no hands.
"Perhaps," she said, staring east while
he kept watch in the west, "the police are right,
the case is closed, sunk out of sight.
When I was a child he told me
stones in the riverbed are fallen angels."

Café Society

Down a flight of stairs to Golövlev's
café door basket-woven with strips of black steel,
damp wood hissing in a stove, the accordionist on a stool.
Her cheeks were white as chestnut candles
in the marbled mirror behind the coffee machine.
Under the petals of an exhaust fan
a waiter set down wedges of lemon, red
caviar and minced whites of hard-boiled eggs.

There was a photograph on the wall,
a legless man in a wheelchair scything weeds
along a gravel road, his stumpy sister behind him
licking butter from a slice of bread.
"What's to be done is we can only promise nothing."
In the cloakroom, a husk of a man shuffled
among empty hangers clasping
his coat tag: "116," he cried,
"my number from Kolyma."

Hogg stood tight-lipped as police in grey mutton hats
thumbed his passport. A waiter put on a painted glove,
a face with blenching eyes, a bent mouth, one tooth.
After twisting the puppet's nose the police
let Hogg go, and then her, up the stairs into a chafing wind,
lips like porcelain, one flick
of the wet tip of her tongue, a detonation, and laughter:
"Don't worry, it's not the cold that kills."

Himmler's Law

...it was a merciless morality...
HEINRICH HIMMLER

The two angels said, "It's time,
there's a kiln of fire in the hourglass,
time to get the killing done."
So Lot led them out of the noon-

day sun in welcome to his tent.
Men with pretty mouths and sulphur in their eyes
from working the bitumen pits
were about to wishbone the angels

from behind. "They're fine,
they're fine, we'll do their ass."
Lot said No, No. They said Yes.
He said: "What am I, an echo?"

and pimp-walked his ponsy daughters,
both betrothed, each in flower.
They dropped their veils but were declined.
"We're not averse to the ladies, Lot,

but as guys we go for the pursed eye
of the poppy in jackal country."
The angels struck them blind
and showed no pity on the morn. None.

They let Lot fold his tent
and incinerated the city. Not just
the unjust but the unborn, every last one.
Lot's wife stood appalled. Abraham,

tasting sweet ash on the breeze, called,
"Most brightly of all burns the hair."
Lot's wife looked back.
At fault in her sorrow,

she was turned to salt.
Lot kept clear of water,
said the coastal cities were unclean, depraved,
and stoked his stove in a scrutty cave

with burnt offerings to his firebug angels.
As for Sodom, "Leave well enough
alone," he said. "It was a merciless morality,
not a crime against humanity."

He refused to grieve. His daughters, bored,
took him drunk to bed
and bore him grand sons.
He heard his name, how it shrunk

on the wind, and a shudder of wings
at his neck. He started to run
but the angels never came,
not for him anyway.

Cold Comfort

Hogg was led up a cobblestone stoop
to a stifling internal transit office,
black iron lace in the windows.
An Osobeast officer wearing puce shoulder-boards
pared his nails to the nub, yelped,

and stubbed his bleeding thumb in a mangy
sponge held on a hammered brass
paten confiscated from a church clamped shut.
"So the cold here cuts you to the quick,
but it's the spring rains that rot

our nerves, all muck, no one gives a fuck."
He had a stainless steel tooth, a mirthless grin.
"You're on the fly," he said, hitching
his eyebrow as he stamped
Hogg's passport with a star snared in a circle.

Sun Dance

A small boy
spread
a square of embroidered
sailcloth
on the paving stones
outside Mikhailovsky Gardens
and
tried to sell Hogg tiny wooden scarecrows
nailed
to a stick.
"They dance if you pull
the string.
I gave them souls
so they glow in the dark."
Hogg held the boy up to the sun
but he swung his legs
and arms
and
screamed,
shielding his eyes.

The Astoria Hotel

At the ping of the bell
a limping porter

doffed his cap to the concierge
who examined Hogg's signature

as if it were tarnished silver,
then shied away, spooked by the sheen

of scar tissue in his eyes.
"Dreams, never names, are lost at sea."

A letter opener on the counter
caught a blade of light spiralling

seven flights of stairwell
to his shuttered room

where he saw her turn naked
from washing her auburn hair

to ask if true love
ever comes true.

The Maiming

"I am for free love face to face
but men here
take us from behind.
I've clawed the air, standing
up against nowhere.
I've watched them
watch me
in the mirror
impaled on splinters
of light.
I felt need, never desire.
Now I see myself in your eyes,
maimed by hope,
afraid
even boredom
will be taken from me."

As Time Goes By

Hogg praised the scent
of apples in her hair
and promised never to forget.
She offered her body bare
for his blessing.
No regrets.
They denied duplicity
by giving
each other
the lie:
I'll love you till I die.

Ambush

A tent of pale light
from the iron storm lamp
on the table
and faded cotton flowers in a lacquered bowl
beside a window sealed shut,
an antique latch of pewter thumbs
wired together.

Over the bed,
an old water-stained engraving
of stone desert lions
staring
at a disappearing star
and his trousers hung on the bedstead's iron trellis.
He folded her
like the sea in linen.
She held her breath, suspicious of the walls,
and the empty light
socket above the door.

As the bed moved beneath them
they heard shuffling feet in the hall, a dry cough,
and she drew away,
ambushed by dread, afraid to call,
touching herself
until a sigh broke
and fell.

Sleepwalker

Hogg sometimes at night wore his overcoat inside-out and tried to walk through the walls of their room. The walls were blue-tinged, multiple contusions. He began to howl at 3 in the AM, mortified at inflicting so much pain on walls that had done nothing but be themselves. The only way she could keep the house quiet was to guide him into a small empty closet, closing the door behind him. He slept absolutely still standing fowl-wise until he woke. On the third morning, he knocked softly, he came out into the room marvelling at how clearly he could see a spider's web from the night before against the window light, 3 flies like planets at the 4th, 6th, and 7th spheres of a universe in conjunction with the bulbous-backed black sun, and he got into bed where he promised she would hear birdsong, not the footsteps of slink-eyed men with dirty fingers. Though only the ghost of himself, he breathed the word into her ear. "Nothing is what it seems. When dark is closing in, it will be light opening up at the seams."

A Stolen Kiss

A thief and his sister
lived in a hut.
She was very beautiful.
Crouching, she kept the fire.
At night, she went to the side of a road
and lay down. Men circled
her still body and then stole a kiss.
Her brother beat them to death
and stole their gold.
But one night a man gave her water from his flask.
The brother beat him but he did not die.
They carried him to the fire
and beat him until his cries fanned the flame.
He grew yellow, his eyes shining.
She lay near him, naked.
He said, "You are a dark flower."
She cradled his face, stole a kiss,
and crept away to kill her sleeping brother.
She came back carrying satchels of gold.
"Don't be afraid," she said.
"We are free."
He fell into the flames,
his arms on fire.

Fire and Water

"My lonely mother said the sun is a fire wheel
and leapt through the hoop,
fleeing on snowshoes
over snow thirty feet deep,
tangled her feet in the tops of trees
where she died
and was found in the spring
reaching for the earth,
her bones glazed by the wind.
My father gave up sulking in the dark,
asked for more vodka and marzipan
at two in the morning,
and quoted Mandelstam:
'The shy speechless sound
of a fruit falling from its tree,
and round about the forest's
silent music, unbroken...'
He went out and reached for the moon
reflected in a quarry pool
and drowned
believing he was born again."

Letters

Every day
she wrote a letter
to no one

about clouds low
in the sky
and rivers when
they're high,

a face with a clock
on its back
and armies put to rout
as they attacked,

a date of birth
that was late
and the men
she loved to hate,

the hours of fun
undone
before they were begun.

The Glass Heart

"Mother made sourdough cookies,
Mongolian girls on the run
with seed-pearl eyes,
feet dipped in sugar,
and then cleaned
our few silver forks
with a chamois cloth as she sat
scrunched by a window staring at shoals of slush
banked in the canal down below palace façades
of madcap buttercup yellow,

the crumpled ice mounting
pink granite docking stairs
pretty as my childhood doll's house
hidden in the closet
beside the stove where father
played chess, alone,
and accused himself of cheating,
sucking his teeth as he circled the board,
each step measured, stealthy,
rancor climbing the branches

of his throat to the dead
cigar between his teeth
as he caught my eye,
a blue rose
in the mirror
where I laughed, laughed and laughed
until he called me his Little Hyena,

wanting to undress my brain,
to see me shivering
with nothing on my mind

but him, the weight of him,
watching, listening,
his hand clamped over my mouth,
clamping down on his cigar
because he could not understand
that laughter is glass
and has bones
that can be broken,
not by sticks and stones
but by names that break your heart."

A Gaunt Note

"...snow-
blind, a skull-
cap of snow on the hill
broken
by a single strand
of steps,
someone gone
and a hungry bird
pecking
seeds
sheathed in ice
prefigures
the effacing of a face.
I don't wish to die,
except the little death
when we lie together,
that incontinence
of light
in my bones
and the sun
swollen between my thighs,
and a gaunt note,
my cry."

Promise of Rain

"Officers of the Ice Palace
died during the war:
Sedelnikov, Chulpenyev, Belov.
Names, ice on the tongue,
silver bells in the mouth,
that's what Tsvetayeva said—

A name, click of a gun, deep sleep.
Grandmother died then, too,
at 101, shrivelled to the size
of a little girl's crib,
calling for her brother who had lost a leg
at Stalingrad, clean

cut above the knee.
He kept it encased in a lead
box in the family crypt,
afloat in embalming oils,
our great-uncle Victor
who visited his leg once a year,
lit a candle, said a prayer,

flaunted his affairs
with young soldiers
in the lobby of Hotel Astoria,
a respected lexicographer who died despised
in the S & M whipping stall
at a military club,

a compassionate man who talked to my father
about evil, how the tear
in a needle's eye
comes from laughter,
how men like Stalin, Himmler, Beria, not only
know the evil they do

but find it wryly amusing
in all its intricacies of device,
the way pulling the wings off butter-
flies is ferociously funny
to queerly strung choir boys.
What else could their defiant sign

WORK MAKES FREE
over the gate of a death camp be
but a joke that only
killers could enjoy.
They knew, they knew, they knew,
and they laughed, he said,

as they laughed at
work, work, the dignity of work
in the work camps of Siberia.
What a joke,
which is how he thought
of his leg,

a length of space
filled with phantom flex,
a twitch, an ache,
resurrected in those stalls,
as he took the lash
so he could lie down

in laughter
at the inexplicable pain
of baseless hatred,
silver bells in his mouth,
ice on the tongue, names:
Sedelnikov, Chulpenyev, Belov."

Osip Mandelstam Moves His Lips

Now I'm dead in the grave, teeth
singing in the zero:
Stalin stabbed the air
and his seraphim in sharkskin suits
dressed me in amulets of electrical

impulse, shredded my nerves
and sat listening to my heart beat,
not the beating
but the silence in between,
eternity atrophied into an ellipse

fondled by the Phrenologist's fat slug fingers,
content in his Kremlin nest
as they took me naked to the final
genuflection and fed my legs
through the scaffold's door of sprung light,

a footloose gaiety just
like Godiva's dance of ankle bells
up the stairs in Leningrad,
O Godiva, goodbye, I'd forgotten,
even when I can't breathe I want to live…

Moving

Snow. Cold fleece on a black day. He found
her at table playing the piano on a paper
keyboard—

"The world is ripe with unsolved problems,"
she said. Paint scaled off the walls. There
was a knock on the door, men wearing coveralls.
"We are the movers.

We've come to move the piano."

All Ears

"When father went away
I locked his bedroom door
but left his radio on
so the police
listening
through the eye
of the black poppy
in the night table vase
would know
nothing is wrong.
But a man broke in,
picked the lock and nailed
the door shut behind him
and not only refuses to go
but won't turn off the radio
or even admit he is in there.
When I told the police
what was going on
they said they could hear
loud and clear
that
nothing is wrong."

x, the Starting Number

Classification of Apartment Claimant
(para. 26, sect.16.16)

1. A family of three, or what was three thereof (including her-self) has the right to an apartment or sections already reduced but accumulated in proportions of 27 + 20 = 47 square metres.

2. Said party claims by law the right to improve conditions (cites Comrade Stalin: "The writer is the engineer of human souls."), but such conditions if granted cannot constitute more than 56 square metres.

3. The claimant wishes to annex (through partial renovation) from apartment 96 on the same floor exactly 17 square metres: 47 + 17 = 64 square metres, completing an apart-ment that would consist of three rooms. The pertinent and applicable statute: "Renovations planned, recorded, com-pleted in a co-operative building or buildings, in accor-dance with the number of member shares (established), will not exceed 56 square metres, separate or inclusive."

4. Since the proposal established exceeds 56 metres, said acquired room is subject to severance, to which all parties agree, leaving 8 square meters attached to apartment 96, sat-isfying all requirements, including the social policy equal-ization principle of 3 (affirming in practice the three stages of dialectical materialism), using *x* as the starting number:

$$\frac{(x + 7 + 10)\,(1000 - 8) - 17}{992}$$

which simplifies to *x*.

A Doll's Nest

"Once, when it was stinging cold
in the zero
weather of hail-scurf
I stepped

into the white light of creation
at the Technical Institute,
a magnesium glow
of wheels within

prayerwheels on fire,
so stifling in the closed airless rooms
I took off my coat,
and another coat,

and another,
down to the skin, the bone,
the flame in a child's eye, mine,
incredulous in the dark,

staring as a rotted tooth
yanked loose
from my grandmother's scream
sank into a wound
to eat its fill."

The Jubjub Bird

Hogg made up a joke
she couldn't understand
about that odd
white light, god's sleight of hand.

Inclined to fright she woke
in the soul's dark night
of the sublime
and said she got the joke:

S O S
in the hourglass
JUBJUB
in the looking glass

but it was no joke that
he knew

caught
in the beak
of a dying bird
as he broke
out of his own
deep sleep
crying
HELP

Hogg Attends a Performance of *The Exile* at Café Tristan Bernard

The curtain rose on the interior of a frontier dacha. The frontiersman sat in front of his fireplace. There was a knock on the door. The exile entered.

EXILE: Whoever you are, have pity on a hunted man. There is a price on my head.

FRONTIERSMAN: How much?

The exile hurried out as the curtain fell.

Snowflake

It began to snow.
"You suspect my silence,
but it is the way I keep my head clear,
wiping each thought
like a small mirror
or antique angel or candlestick.
The small things
men kill for I clean:
it's all we can do, especially with wounds."
A child took a snowflake on his tongue.
"He's swallowed a tear,
his life has begun."

Hogg Meets Isaac Babel

"What's to be done?" Hogg asked
an old watchman
wearing a quilted jacket outside a welding shop.
"We've been walking in circles for hours
trying to find Tolstoi."

The old man, staring at the back
of his bare hand severed at the wrist
by a black cuff, clucked on his pipe
and scraped his boot on a broken curb.

"He turned yellow, your count. Afraid.
His religion was all fear, frightened
by the cold, by old age, by death. And,
he made a warm overcoat
out of his faith."

The watchman, smelling of savory
and sunflower oil, opened his hand
as if it were a map.
She touched the long life line
and lifted his fingers to her lips.
"He's from the purges, when all was permitted."

He let her kiss his hand.

The Old Believer

The lunatic Old Believer
cut adrift
from his mother's thighs
leapt out of the luminous sty

with visions
in his seraphic eye
of Streltsi
crucified

on crosses
anchored to the sky
where
death was only dross

redeemed
through Christ's cry.
"Goodbye, goodbye to the slaughter.
They know not

what they do
with these rows of empty shoes
and so forgive them,
Little Father."

Great Peter

On his long spindly legs,
six-foot-nine
in silk stocking feet,
he mocked his own marriage
by mating dwarfs,
supplied monks with a lifetime of fleas
and filled in the swamps with drowned men.
He took a German mistress,
Anna Mons, to her knees,
and put aside his wife, Avdotia,
who pronounced a curse:
"This place shall be empty..."
as he hunched under the low ceiling
of his chartroom,
studying construction plans
for canals and the cochineal and ochre
façades of palladian palaces
imported from Tuscany,
stopping only to
pour pearls
from a quiver into his son's lap.
"Dreams are born in little deaths," he said.
"Life makes sense in sacrifice."
He throttled the boy,
infanticide his patrimony
as he paraded the child's corpse
between hayricks stacked with skulls,
the stench of decay on the downwind.

Hogg Goes to the Movies

It was a silent crowd, silent as all the book stores were silent. The film was in black and white, a story in gritty shadow with lashings of ivory light. At mid-point a man who is bald from fear because he has been screwing the roly-poly wife of his boss—and she has forced him to screw her, threatening to turn him in as a turncoat—is standing in a telephone booth that is all glass. He is talking, eyes darting, but his words cannot be heard as he looks over his shoulder and looks and looks. But he does not see what the audience sees: A giant crane has swung overhead and the lowering pincers of a cherry picker pluck the booth and man, his scream a silence behind glass, up into the air. The crane wheels out over the calm bay on a soft summer's day and drops the telephone booth. It makes no entry splash, only a ruffle of water around the hole. Someone in the dark of the theatre called out, "Ten. A perfect ten." The audience roared and then roared with laughter again as the waters settled into an absolute stillness, the man, the booth, sunk out of sight. It was the second roar that left Hogg so rattled until supper when he insisted on making wordless love standing up by the sink until she cried out, her mouth twisted by joy, his anger swealing away.

Amputated Love

Death is the only cure for the hunchback.
NIKITA KHRUSHCHEV

Hogg met a man with silverfish eyes
in the glacial sheen
who said he'd wiretapped his son's dream
and heard the broken voice

of a boy soprano
whose only choice
was a rainbow
radioactive in his entrails

or queuing for aminazine
in psychiatric jails.
He had the eloquence
of amputated love

bewildered by pain
dangling in an empty glove
and the acid rain
in his son's life sentence.

"How," he cried,
"do I apologize before he dies?"

Khishchuk and Ugolov, 1984:
A Legal Fragment

In the early morning two battalion foot soldiers assisted officers Maxim Khishchuk and Victor Ugolov in the unprovoked killing of enemy children. These officers, sportsmen, were trap-shooting with double-barrelled shotguns. Their foot soldiers flung babies of regional women into the air as the officers had instructed and cried, according to civilian witnesses, Pull-BLAM. Re-crank. Pull-BLAM. Re-crank. Over the course of an hour, Khishchuk in direct hits outscored Ugolov and secured a wager they had made that morning, that is, Khishchuk's obligation as winner to shoot Ugo-lov and then kill himself. Khishchuk did. The two foot soldiers gathered twenty of the scattered dead and built a pyre in a pumpkin field preparing to burn the bodies after rolling a gasoline drum forward through the vines, but superior officer Valentin Felikosovich Voino-Belyayev shot the two soldiers dead. Voino-Belyayev was convicted of dereliction of duty for not supervising his sub-officers, and also with murder in the case of the two soldiers, whose adjutant argued successfully that they were carrying out orders, which they had done with diligence and dispatch. The foot soldiers' families were granted half pensions. Voino-Belyayev, accorded leniency, was sentenced to ten years of reconstructive re-education in a corrective labour camp because *the heart of the matter is not personal guilt, but social danger;* he asked to be blindfolded instead before a firing squad but his anti-social request was denied. He was transported in leg chains. The dead were buried in an unmarked grave. Our battalion retreated, leaving the inevitable in crement of victims to the pumpkin field.

The Wound

"Sometimes I think
the hem of light
under a kitchen door
is an inch or two of respite,
Akhmatova
breaking bread on a table,
keeping the room clean
as a wound
that will not heal:
*one day the age will rise
like a corpse in a spring river.*"

So It Is Said

In this hour
of lead
a child
beaten
down like a dog
got up
like a man
only
to be
shot
and blown
legless
in an unknown
bog
as his
general
lay dying
in the
leisure
of
his bedroom
not only
untroubled
by life
as a
temporary
measure

but
stroking
the bloom
of a
siberian iris
sent
by
his aide-de-camp.

Champagne

Six black men seated
under an old MIG propeller
bracketed into a ceiling sprocket
were shouting in a corner:
Lenin, Lenin, Lenin.
"Slogans and spittle,"
the barman sneered, sending tulip
glasses of local champagne
to the table of drunken Africans,
ANC students on scholarship
who carried ice picks in their belts,
"For shucking Baltic oysters," they yelled,
hoisting the pink underpants of a streetgirl
who'd taken two of them to bed
for 40 dollars and a carton of Camels.
"We are all spiders
sculpting air in a bottle,"
the barman said as he ladled
Hogg's steaming cabbage soup into a bowl,
"but in your country
bottles are washed so clean
you press your nose to the glass
and believe you are free.
What more can a man ask?"
The Africans cranked their
SONY short-wave radio,
snatching McCartney and Lennon
singing "Back in the U.S.S.R."
out of the air
and called for more champagne.

Heartbeat

After a fall of wet snow
a man trudging in a circle cried,
"It's for the throat, a necklace
not a noose."
They turned in to a stone-paved courtyard,
her narrow rooms off Glinka Street,
and sat at a small parquet table,
dried spring flowers and postcards from Odessa
pressed under glass.
The phone rang.
No one was there, the line dead.
"During the siege my grandmother's ivory-inlaid metronome
was propped by one of the symphony's second violinists
before an open microphone
at the radio station
so if Shostakovich stopped
the nation would know
we were still alive by the
tock tock tock."
She laid out mätjes herring on a plate
but wouldn't eat,
arranging old family photographs
in a ring on the floor.
"Sitting in the centre of all this
I can hardly breathe.
I love you like I love God.
I can't believe you're here."

Foundling

"When I was little
I lost my name
in the snow.
It was a cold day, so cold
I left fingerprints
in the air,
afraid
I might disappear,
but father kissed my hands
and said,
'There's nothing
to fear,
they have lists and lists
of names
and the evidence
is there,
they'll find you.'"

Cradle Song

During a freakish thaw
wood ash settled like pollen
on the window pane,

the sun became more
than a red welt
on the sky's rim,

and in the ice-bound river basin
albino eels
began to melt.

She split an apple from pole to pole,
prying the seed cup,
cradle of generation

swallowed up in regeneration,
and said, "I used to dream happily
of escape on the ice floes

and burial at sea,
but now I want us naked
in a meadow of feathers."

Christa: A Miracle

A
crosstree
of
two
planks
came apart
in
shifting
ice
as he hauled
her down
into
his arms.
She felt
nails ease
out of her flesh
and
her
wounds
healing.

Bluebeard

As she cleared
her window sill
of snow with a whisk,
a jar of plastic
daffodils on the ledge,
Hogg flew her father's black kite
in the courtyard.
She said it looked like a spider
in the sky's ear
listening for a voice
on the other end of the line,
but he said, No, no, I am flying
one of the annealed
angel's charred wings.
He promised
to find real flowers
by late afternoon, perhaps
a pot of eyebrights.

Rasputin

I

He took the universe personally.
 He beat his father about the ears
and cast by telegraph a healing spell
on the tsarina's son.
Drunk, he stripped down to his stink,
scabies and eau de cologne, and whipped
the naked Olga Lokhtina,
wife of a Petersburg general,
as a concertina played and she held him
by his cock, crying out, "You are God!"
He jammed the whip between her teeth.
"Only love is holy."

II

Wearing a crown of lice
he had stolen from an old priest
he went out for a skate on the midnight ice.
He had eyes like snaked dice,
but with the coercive charm of a scrupulous sinner
who has nothing to hide he disarmed
Hogg, taking him by the arm, and stride
by stride they sped down the canal
on a lonely bacchanal.

"I was a tongue of fire
spurned by insipid sanctifiers
and generals who turned the sabbath host
black with death counts
only they could live with.
I haunted the holy ghost.

I sacrificed myself to sin.
The scourge, the rutting was all for Him.
Just as He chose to die for me
cankered in my skin,
I chastened souls till they became His sluts.
I repented and am consoled."

Lovesick

She leapt out of bed
and saw from behind
the white blind
two bare broken
feet poking through the tailgate
of a truck carting septic
tanks and spools of barbed
wire to an army barracks.
"Remember Golövlev's café,
the touch of your tongue,
my coat fell open,
I was blue with cold
in a fever-sweat for days
wondering who you were,
your long fingers
stroking my neck, spent
like someone
hanged must be,
sprung free
into a cure
for death,
eternity.
I live in a sick country,
I am a sick woman,
I'll love my country
till the day I die."

What Voznesensky Whispered to Hogg

They
can hang
light bulbs
by
a vinyl
cord

but
the poet
hangs
by
his
spinal
chord

WANTED: A POPOV MACHINE

(hand-painted sign on the Street Corner of Mimes)

Among acro-
bat freedom
fighters, a juggler, a rope-
dancer, clowns, a pup-

                                          pet police-
             man who opens a door
                 to his chest and takes
                    out a secret police-

man pretending
to be a marionette with
a face of wax who
is hanged from

                                  a lamppost
                    in effigy of Socrates
               who sleeps suspended
                      in air dreaming

of a flower on fire
inside the lung
of the mime as he becomes
a flute, becomes the hol-

                            low of his own back-
                        bone, fingering
                 the sound of an ab-
                       solute silence

completed by
the criss-crossing of his
feet and applause
from the cupped hands of the dangling cop   *clop, clop, clop*

A Mute Chord

He'd sing to her of the good
true and beautiful if only he saw God
absolute in the scarecrow's pod.

Instead, he hears assonance in atrocities,
the wise fool for revolution
condemned to eternal detention
in a death-
defying
dance of insane
elegance,

his tumbling cry
a mute chord
at the feet
of man's effigy,
Our Lord,
the
Word.

Wishboned

At midnight she made a wish on his body
and began to dream
of sleeping till the end of time:—
the drip drip
of blood
in the hourglass stopped,
whipping stalls stood empty,
only the stain remained
as men ladling stars
from root cellars
saw aureolas appear
around their eyes, a promise of rain,
and fear big as sails
took flight.
In still waters
she lay waiting
to never wake up.
It was unbearable,
like waiting
for a child to drown.
At dawn,
she began to scream.

Mon Grand Guignol

"Then there was my acrobat.
Tall and double-jointed, he could bend his body
in a circle backwards and hold on to his heels
so that a clown wired like an angel
with little wings could jump hoop through him.

He'd call to me upside down from between his legs,
'One day we'll wheel within a wheel into the sun.'
He skipped rope, too, on a high wire,
double-dutch, cavorting with the clown,
but the army plucked him out of the air

and parachuted him into the Afghan hills.
He blew off a leg to a land mine and came home
looking for himself in our bedroom mirror
but got lost in the silver lining.
Out of sight, he went out of his mind,

tried to tighten the letter O around his neck, his rope,
his skipping rope, but then crawled into an asdic hut
salvaged from an arctic submarine hunter
that sits rusting under Petrovski bridge where Rasputin
had been wormed half-dead through a hole in the ice.

Every morning he stands there on his hands
and talks down through the crust to the beard,
bared gums, and crazed healing eyes of the holy man jacking
the ice with all his might, trying to come up for air.
On clear days the acrobat bends his body backwards.

He holds on with two hands to his one heel. He waits.
But the circle is broken. 'O', he cries. 'O'. The clown never comes.
Sometimes he stands on his good leg
like a crane and wheels his out-
stretched arms, trying to take off."

At the Beach

As old pipes in the apartment walls clanked,
she drew steaming bath water
from the overhead tank
so Hogg could kneel
in the clouds
and wash her
in the clawfoot tub.

A tear trickled
down the crackled tiles like the shining trail
of a cockled snail.

Wearing only a Sputnik souvenir cap
won at a Young Pioneers Pic-Nik
for knowing all the names
of cosmonauts
who'd flown in outer space,
she stared out to where
she thought Helsinki might be
and then tested
the scalding sea with her toe.

"When it gets so hot I can't breathe
I will know
love is a mouthful
of water ice-cold
as hell frozen over."

The White Fairy Tale

Virgin snow fell during the night. The world
was white. So white the white snow goose laid a white egg,
losing it in the snow. The white rooster's
white song flew under the eaves
and froze, an icicle long in the tooth.
The white squirrel sired white
squirrels who leapt onto white branches,
and the squirrel lost them.

Hogg reeled in a white
pike and found the ark's white dove
alive in the stomach. He tied a note to the dove's tail
and she flew off. "If she finds you,
feed her. Don't let the police clip her wings
and every evening warm her belly
with a white water bottle.
Write if she lays a golden egg!"

Sky Queen

"I carried a bottle of rainwater
out to the root cellar
to sit among empty seedling trays.
It was chilling, the lathing
bare, caulking broken.
There were dunes
of dust from carpenter ants
in the corners.
Neighbours believe a stillborn child
is cocooned under the stone paving,
son of a Potemkin sailor,
his winding sheet cut from an admiralty flag.
I sipped my water,
tepid but pure, tasting of lilacs.
The child talked to me,
discreetly,
of fields of stars,
the blue of the moon
and how you would come.
The sky was at my feet."

Tell It Slant

"Eclipse,
eclipse, there is
no wafer
of light, no light:
we drool over light
in our dreams, seize the day
in the dark
and try to live
as we're going to die,
with no time
to waste.
It is who we are,
fair-skinned,
black bones and heart.
We atone, we
atone, persisting in the sin
of doing nothing
but exist
and we inoculate
our lives
with alcohol.
We come home
listening
for the padded
step in the stairwell.
We are laconic, erect
on the grave's lip."

Hogg in the Land of H.

Unhinged on vodka 96 point 6,
he eyeballed the bottom of his glass
and called out a childhood game.
"I spy with my little eye
a place that begins with the letter H."
He leaned into the glass
for a gimlet look and saw a lake
with a thousand thousand windows in the water.
He opened one and went out into the dark
where he saw
a tall man,
himself, who stood so tall
he was clearing the sky of cranes
with a rake. Marina buried
the birds as soon as they crashed and drove
stakes into the heart of each grave
so that no one could ever rise from the dead.
"And so, the State will wither away."
Hogg, thumbs in his eyes,
pushed back tears.
He wanted blindness,
in this blind
pig of a place
under the letter H.

A Blown Kiss

"The sky hadn't left the ground for a month
and mother, who kept dried petals
between the pages of her bedside books,

cut off the heads of six daisies. She buried
the yellow-eyed blooms in jars
of glycerine granules that sucked out

all the moisture and quoted Tsvetayeva:
'What is love? It is a flower
flooded with blood.'

My mother had taught me to braid
the cut stems into a whisk
for egg whites and bowls of flour

pulped from potatoes.
I told her: 'Bleeding is not love,
love is *one* artichoke leaf eaten by *two* people.'

Armoured half-track carriers
clanked under the kitchen window.
She snapped the book shut. 'Artichokes,

artichokes are no more, they'll be
forgotten. Dictionary entries will read—
obsolete!' A tiny white flower fell

from our bedside Tsvetayeva to her lap.
She put one dry petal to her lips,
kissed it, and blew."

Her Mother

"Though the dressing rooms were shabby
there were still chandeliers
of cut crystal, gilt mirrors,
and women sprawled against the tiled walls,
naked, their stomachs glistening.
Our cracked shoes were stacked
in wire racks,
and one old woman
always came from the market
carrying onions
in a stocking hung over her shoulder.
She doused herself
with pails of cold water, and the young girls, too,
who mistakenly thought she was mean.
You could not fool the old ones,
they flicked lies
from the air with their tongues,
huddled around the cast-iron heater
and promised love lasts longer
in the salt of unshed tears.
The air was sour with steaming wool.
Sometimes when the masseuse braided my hair
I felt the future
flickering
behind me in an oval mirror,
but when I turned
I saw only the broken smile
of my mother."

Stasis

"Wait, we stand in line waiting
for sugar, squeaky rubber shoes,
we wait in line lined-up for the lineup for toilet
rolls, wait for a single lemon, the telephone's
stunned silence on the other end to end,
to sleep in shifts, shiftless,
while we wait for toothpowder,
power blackouts, kohl to raccoon our eyes
and tampons twice a year, waiting
that is so inlaid in our lives
it must be police policy as we wait
at office doors for inter-
office times to be posted
by inter-office officials who wait
for us so dead-tired from doing
nothing we can do
nothing but wait…"

Orphans

"My father often sat in candlelight,
his sleeves stained by wax,
and while he played the shadows
of his hands
like charred wings on the wall,

mother played a black flute with silver stops,
a gift from her cross-eyed lover
who had become a translator from the Chinese
in a border town beyond Lake Baku.
'It was either that for him or repair bicycles.'

She laid the flute in a drawer
with ladles, spoons and his letters written on rice paper:
'He says he hears a constant ringing
in his ears, the wheels of cattle cars
on feeder lines to a re-education camp.'

My father, aggrieved because
he ate every night with a woman
he no longer slept with, snuffed the flame with his fingers.
'We should holiday in Prague or Bratislava or Berlin,
except it's already past nine o'clock, too late, too late to go.'

He unlatched the window and leaned into the clear night air.
'This afternoon,' he said, 'I bicycled
beside a girl with one green eye,
the other stung blind in a machine shop,
who said she only needed one
to see how cruel we've all become.'

He stood watching smoke
curly-Q from little tin-roofed
chimney pots across the alley.
She made black tea in an enamel bowl
and spoke in a whisper of egg

whites whisked to a weightless foam
and eating artichokes *two* to *one* leaf.
He closed the window.
'I got a whiff on the wind
of everybody who's been orphaned.'"

Homesick

"She knelt
beside her wedding bed
clearing
a cedar hope chest.

She looked into the palm
of her hand, saw
the life line disappearing, closed her
fist and held on to what she had,

a tortoiseshell barrette
that she laid on the bedspread
beside a lilac sachet,
a rhinestone choker, a glass ball

thick with falling snow
and grandmother's capsules
of holy water from Novgorod,
never opened.

Homesick in her house,
mother got constriction of the heart
from lying in his bed
in search of a cure."

At the Winter Palace

I

Six winged horses
suspended in slow step
over the cobbled square,
a muscled sea nymph
primed in a bed of porcelain
for the nuptial feast where
cowled women gathered serpents' eggs
and acorns were poured from
a boyar's helmet—
he twirled his moustache,
brushed a sapphire bloom of snow
from the sleeve
of a prince orphaned by war
and said, "Here is happiness,
a little ice on the wind."

II

In the enamelled skull
of the holy man who had served
that prince: a votive flame,
socketed testimony
of how he'd sought evidence
against himself,
how he had
worn a shirt of lice
and immolated his lust in ice
and left one written sign, XB,
his death words
in stained glass:
When snow weeps,
a child will laugh.

A Little Piece of the Night

"On a clear day in a cul-de-sac
of skeletal trees my prancing father
flew a little piece of the night, his black kite,
pretending he was a circus horse.

I told my mother. She unlocked
the dew-lap hinge to grandfather's regimental
case (the pistol lost) and removed
a pair of yellow kid riding gloves soft

still to the touch. As a cavalry officer
he had cantered through Crimea and Orlau
but had refused to ride roughshod over hymn-singing steel
workers at the Winter Palace. Four years

later, denounced by his brother
as a *Trotskiticha* and, ordered to mount a defence,
he skittered from stall to stall
in the Company stable, halting to shout

into his horse's ear: 'We could of course lose patience.'
At dawn, he disembowelled the general's dappled
grey, was arrested and court-martialled.
'My evil brother dost love me,' he cried, 'I love

my brother,' as he stood on parade, boots
reversed in the stirrups, stripped of shoulder pips
and membership in the Party. His wife wept, blinked, hic-
cuped, fell off the edge of a chair

screwing her thumbs into her ears
and went down crouched like someone hunting
lost shoes in the subway and never came back.
He stood stolid sentry at the escalator.

'She'll rise up, you'll see, or what's death for?'
Officers, adjutants, his harelipped brother
disappeared. He flattened a city map
on the kitchen table, frazzled

from eating only crushed walnuts sprinkled over
pumpkin porridge. He enlarged
the underground, the charts, inscribing sub-
stations in ever-decreasing circles so crowds

of accused could link up down below, move
freely. 'But if this keeps on,' he said,
'the country will collapse, implode, it's a sink-hole.'
There was no opening for air on the map.

All black. He cloaked himself in a cavalry
blanket, went down the escalator, leaving behind
his kid gloves which I wear on my namesake day,
and the map my father primed

with linseed oil and made into a black kite.
Once a year pretending he is a horse he prances
and lets the kite loose from that cul-de-sac,
flying a little piece of the night."

Fathers & Sons

I

Stones lose their wings
and lie
in common ground,
wear a crown of earth.
Men
spill common seed,
dream their sons as stars
who never die.

II

Stars, stars,
falling stars, shooting stars,
they make no noise,
not a sound we ever hear
though we all lie
down
with our ear
to the ground
as they disappear.

A woman
blinking in the sunlight
boasted, "I own this, I own this,"
as she thrust

a long wooden spoon and child's bib
stained red by borscht
into Hogg's face,
chucking him under the chin.

"But it may be blood. Yes, blood.
Do you know, did you read, it was only after the flood,
after Noah saved them, two by two,
that men began to eat meat?

Still, some have come through,
one by one."
She told Hogg to keep
an eye peeled for her only son.

"He was wearing a rust-coloured raincoat,
but you never know who to trust,
people drown on sunny days
and think nothing of it."

Hogg crossed under the cobalt spire
of the Church of Transfiguration
and found a shivering man
walking naked on his knees around

a weeping birch.
"There's ex-cons on the Nevsky," he said,
"guttersnipes, deadbeats, leeches,
who say they only steal because Stalin stole their lives,

so they up and snatched my salted
herring and green tomatoes,
three old *zeks* who had gone down for tenners
in the high tundra camps,

thugs who threatened to feed
my balls to a corn-shucking machine
and then accused me, my green seeds
dribbling down their chins,

of blackmarketeering, calling for the cops
who came in 2s, total of 6,
and then 6, and another sneering 6,
to strip-search my Jew's ass, they said, and torch my transit papers,

leaving me nowhere here with no name,
but then they gave me *bupkes*, it was all a joke, they said,
the convicts were killing time,
not me."

Hunger

Surrounded by elms swollen with snow
our soldiers dug in during the December siege of '42
and ate cattle-cakes and boiled carpenter's glue
and froze to death in anti-tank ditches
refusing to cut ancestral trees for firewood.
"Children starved in their father's arms.
I die in yours,
You are someone from nowhere
I know nothing about."
A truck drove by half-loaded with drowsy pigs
followed by a skimming bird
pecking at ticks
plump with blood.
"When you undo my blouse you undo my bones,
like a king who sucks the toes
of his slaves,
you feed me your own hunger."

An Evening Drive

They went with her agèd uncle, Colonel Blobel.
She hardly knew him
but Hogg was invited to dinner too,
so they went together.
It was evening and just getting dark.
At one moment—they were driving
past a long ravine—Hogg noticed strange
movements of the earth: clumps
of clay rose into the air
as if by their own propulsion—
and there was smoke: it was like
a low-toned volcano
as if there was burning
lava just beneath the earth.
Blobel laughed, made a gesture
with his arm, pointing back
along the road and ahead:
"Here lie my 30,000."

The Eyes Have It

Cousin Smerdikov, a sharp-
shooter, a Grepo garrisoned at the Berlin wall for two years
in a tin-roofed concrete bunker,
shinnied up the courtyard drain pipe
carrying a knapsack of stolen carp
into her cramped kitchen.
A deserter on the grift, agile, ingratiating,
he kept a live sparrow
in his breast pocket, both wings broken.
It hip-hopped on the old harvest
table, overfed, plump,
peep peep peeping
as she scooped eyes of potatoes on to a plate,
asking Hogg whether he thought carp
with their old priest's whiskers
ever smiled in the dark water
before taking the bait.
"Bottom feeders," Smerdikov said,
talking about the security police,
how they had the look
of drowned men.
The bird ate the eyes.

The Note

…What gives value to travel is fear. It is the fact that, at a certain moment, when we are so far from our own country…we are seized by a vague fear, and the instinctive desire to go back to the protection of old habits. At that moment we are feverish but also porous, so that the slightest touch makes us quiver to the depths…so we should not say that we travel for pleasure. There is no pleasure in travelling, and I look upon it as an occasion for spiritual testing. Pleasure takes us away from ourselves in the way that distraction, as in Pascal's use of the word, takes us away from God. Travel, like a greater and graver science, brings us back to ourselves…

Passports

At nine in the morning
by the dashboard
clock, there was an acrid
mildew on the air, not dew.
Pyotr Mikhailovich, Hogg's driver, *shapka* earflaps
tied at the back of his neck,
ate a cold potato he'd been carrying in his pocket.

"So me and the boys, I was ten in '41,
we skinned our eyes as troopers
drove up in tarpaulined trucks,
it was October, all clammy and drizzle,
an anti-tank ditch angled up to the highway,
hundreds were stripped to their stupid underwear

and machine-gunned, they puked up blood
and left their litter of money pouches,
sheepskin coats—all the sleeves
yanked inside out—blanket rolls
tied with twine, hand-carved
decoy ducks and a cage with a canary
pecking at himself in a mirror

while conscripts skunked on the local
slosh of cranberry jam and vodka in a jar
sifted through the jumbled passports
and stamped all names CANCELLED and drew huge
tits around the ID eyes in photos.
By dusk they'd heaved
all the bodies into the pit

but under the bull-
dozed earth some heard
muffled singing and I saw fingers
of blue smoke seep up between loose
clumps of mud and shale.
Then the ditch collapsed like a lung."

Tear

"After every storm,
children
offer me handfuls
of hail,
souls of men
sheathed
In Ice.
I eat their sins,
though it's so cold
and sunless
here
the dead
steal their own bones
for firewood
They know the bead of light
in a pterodactyl's bill-hook
is
God's
only tear."

All Found

She slipped off a shoe,
saw a hole in the toe
of her stocking
and began to cry.
"When I was a girl my father
said I had a pretty face,
told me to hide it in his suitcase
so he could spy on me.
I tried to disappear,
to slip up someone's sleeve,
but always, always he was there,
with his hands mussing my hair,
his kiss a smear
across my heart,
smooth as the two stones
I toyed with in my fist,
click click click,
a secret code that allowed me to forget
everything but the sound,
click click click.
Click.
Until you came,
I was nowhere here to be found."

A Cold Child

Outside Troubetzkoy Bastion
the guard's varnished boots shone
as he barked his heels to attention.
A girl wheeling
an empty pram laughed.
"Peter killed his son here.
We all carry a cold child, no good
at anything except suffering
and telling lies to enhance
the truth."
Her husband, tugging his *shapka*
as if trying to placate
some apparatchik, wagged his head, saying,
"No no not that it's not true,
though maybe yes, so maybe no."
The guard sucked air through his teeth.
"Says who?" he sneered
and spun on his heel.

Trumps

When her mother saw
a dressmaker's dummy
hanged from a guardrail,
seagulls staining the wire chassis,

she cried, "But that is me," and cursed
a policeman cupping cold water from a tap
to his pocked cheeks.
"Why didn't you protect me?

Or at least cut me down?"
Pulling out a soft packet
of Lucky Strikes he'd bought
that morning on the black market,

he asked to see her photo-ID.
"That's not you," he said.
"You'd better be gone
by the time I count to three."

She played an evening game of whist
with her doctor, a heart specialist,
who tried to tamp her rage down

by telling her she had exquisite breasts
for a woman her age.
"Still the shape of a champagne glass."

She snorted, pounded her fist,
bid one heart, was trumped by diamonds
and buried on a clear and crisp morning

after coughing blood all night.
Her seamstress cut loose the skeleton
and winged a stone at the birds

but could shed no light, no word,
on who had stolen the bones.
Her mouth was full of pins.

A Bird Peeped

They were unassuming men—
a pediatrician,
film projectionist and beadle,
a sausage stuffer, a local marriage broker, an usher
with gold crowns on the brain
who prayed for overcast nights but no rain.
With bayonets, spades, and picks,
they sweated and snuffled,
rags smeared across their mouths,
and complained the skeletons
were in heaps of tangled arms and legs.
Two putty-eyed men with axe handles
caved in skulls and cranked out
teeth with pliers by the light
of highbeams, afraid their batteries
would snuff before the slur of first light.
They drove to the thieves' market
beyond the marsh to haggle
with Valdemiers the appraiser who
wore rubber gloves, afraid of infection.
He rinsed his jeweller's
glass in vinegar and complained about *krysha*,
the protection money he coughed up
to security police. Smerdikov the sharpshooter's
drawstring pouch was plugged full of gold teeth,
several good-sized molars.
His bird peeped in his breastpocket.

Tricksters

"We all live with a lie
up our sleeve,
officers carry a leather wand
to make men disappear,
whole towns, villages.
Deception comes so easily,
we have changed wine
back to water again.
We are good at what we do.
Only the dove
refuses
to come out
of his hat."

How Would You Feel?

The Simferopol Action: Case No. 1586:
Anton Smerdikov "...systematically purloined
articles of jewellery from the burial
place at the 10th kilometre.
On the night of June 21, disregarding moral
norms, he did purloin from the aforesaid grave
a gold pocket-watch case weighing 35,02 grams
calculated at 27 rubles 30 kopecks
per gram, a gold bracelet of 30 grams
worth 810 rubles—the whole valued
at 3325 rubles 68 kopecks...on June 13
he stole gold crowns and bridges,
to a total value of 21,925 rubles,
a gold ring of 900 carats with a diamond
worth 314 rubles 14 kopecks, four chains
to the sum of 1360 rubles, a gold ducat
of foreign coinage worth 609 rub. 65 kop.,
89 coins of the Tsar's coinage worth
400 rub. Each (vol. 2, pages 65-70)."
Hogg asked Smerdikov the sharpshooter:
"What's it feel like down there, digging?"
He replied: "How would you feel,
yanking out a kid's shoe
with a bit of a foot in it?"

Home Fires

"My father's father
had given him a regimental
tie, a straight razor
with a bone handle, a worn strop,
and a stainless-steel cigarette lighter
with Stalin's profile on the flip-top lid.

He bared his teeth in a loving smile,
his breath smelling of the anise seeds
he swallowed to sweeten his lies
as he gave me the cigarette lighter.

He touched me, fondled
me, between the legs,
mother turning a slant
eye at the door.

I told him Stalin was a shit."

Stigmata

A young lawyer
copying
testimony from yellowing trials

into an oilcloth notebook
squinted in the pale light
of the unwashed Registry windows

and thrust his damp
cheek close to Hogg's chin.
"No citizens, none are noted here. Absolutely

none. After all, citizens ask questions.
These accused came into court
only to condemn themselves,

shambling indolent men like
this Boris Samoilov, look
how indolent in his own defence,

line 4, files 3892 and 1769.
Born, date unknown, Petrograd.
Shop assistant. Arrested, 23 May, 1976. Referred—

to the archives of Vakhtin Clinic,
kneading (they all did, you see it
in photographs from the time) the open

abscess of accusation in his hand,
eager to verify every lie
he testified to as true,

trying not to die, not to die, not to die.
Preposterous. Can you imagine
a life with no death?

Absolutely not.
Without dying there's no God,
without God, no hope

and we believe in both
though we say we don't."
He cropped

the air with a sign
of the crucifix,
scratched his itchy crotch, and laughed.

"It's all the same to me.
Burning, scalding, stench, consumption,
fie! fie! fie! pah! pah!"

The Acrobat

In a decrepit cathedral
that had been used
as a warehouse, the pillars strung with tackle
and flywheels,
a magician sawed several soldiers in half.
They rose, releasing pigeons.
Bears unicycled in a circle
while a tightrope walker eased along the latitude of fear.
He suddenly disappeared,
scaling a ladder straight into the air.
The master of ceremonies
who did cipher work
two nights a week for the KGB,
searching for graves that had been buried, called,
"Come down, there's nowhere to go up there."
Lights scissored the dark
until they pinned him to the ceiling
in a wafer of white.
Slovo i dielo, he cried,
and dived with his arms wide
into a safety net.
Women in the crowd wept
and clowns flopped on their backs
imitating the acrobat
until children laughed and the crowd sang
a local komsomol song,
Even the horse doesn't need the whip.

Hogg on 96 Point 6

On a plain chair
he sat down drunk with one eye
open trying to locate the lame
pallbearer who had been dogging him

as he sat down
on a plain chair and crossed
a short right leg over what felt like his long left
trying to find ground zero, his toes,

as he sat down
on a plain chair, mirthless no matter
how loud he laughed, and cried,
"Don't worry 'bout the horse being blind,"

as he sat down
on a plain chair, "just load up the wagon,"
feeling as empty from the dry heaves
as the hat he held on to in his lap

as he sat down
on a plain chair and teetering saw that he
could no longer see and fell asleep before
hitting the floor, still wary, with one eye open.

Hogg All Found

With one eye
blue, the other brown,

the earth at sea,
the sea ran aground,

then the other way
around as the moon

came down to earth.
His blue eye turned

brown, the brown blue,
and the sea turned, too.

So grace abounds
in what was lost

and now is found
in the round.

Hogg Is Accosted
by a Former Dance Instructor
Now One-legged
Who Is Moonlighting as a Juggler

He stood propped by a peg-leg crutch with a top hat down by his toes as he called out, "Such was the revolution," and juggled two balls, one red, one white, and then two more, and two more till there were three x three in the air. Then the balls fell one-by-one into the hat till the air was clear and he flipped the hat and three red balls bounced into his broad coat pocket. The white ones had disappeared. He said as he put the hat on his head, "All is lost, you know, but nothing goes to waste," and he began to hop in a circle with a word popping out of his mouth at each leaping clop of his one-legged shoe in the snow: air, air, air, air, air, air, air, air

Phoenix

Ivarr the Boneless,
bivouacked on the shore
of the White Sea,
pocketed a small stone
and warmed it in his hand
all the way home
to his garrison
south
of Lake Ladoga.

In a fit of anger
he had the stone sewn
into the mouth
of a spy,
the body beheaded,
burned,
and the face with its pursed mouth
fired
from a catapult
into the Dark Wood

where it was found
by a blond horseman,
his breast painted blue,
who hung the head
by the hair over his hearth,
and waited for it to speak.

The thread dried,
broke,
and the stone leapt out
into the fire pit.
He raked the coals
until the stone
cracked.
A black serpent
stood
in the flame—
flute,
flowering stem,
the hooded priest's
backbone,

coiling
into a bracelet of
ash,
a name in smoke,
Ivarr the Boneless,

and wearing a winged helmet
he rode south to the Black Sea
to redeem the world
by war if
needs be.

The Golden Egg

On board the battle cruiser *Kronverk*, anchored and converted to a café of supper table snugs, waiters set down devilled eggs stippled with caviar and bottles of Starorusskaya encased in blocks of ice. "This crowd is KGB," she said. Two dancers stutter-stepped in strobe lights as a magician levered a liquored-up section chief by the lapel into a circle of nine mirrors reflecting a door reflecting doors that were not glass anymore but a corridor. The chief cried, "Help." The room went dark and he cried "Help" again, the silence sinister as poisoned bread. Then, in a risen light the mirrors were gone, the chief, too. The magician pulled a golden egg from Hogg's astonished mouth, cracked it open, and handed him a tiny stone and slip of paper.

> *To our love of pain be true*
> *by walking with this stone*
> *in your shoe.*

Bruegel's Two Monkeys
(her dream)

An interim interrogation, another final exam:
two chained monkeys sitting in a window,
the sky fluttering in the wind
the sea bathing itself.

Mankind's humanity moot?
She stammers through words.

One monkey cocks a wry ear in disdain,
the other seems bone-weary—
but when silence ensues after each query
he prompts her
with a slight rustling of his chain.

In a Minor Key

"Do you believe I could have opened
my arms to you
without embracing them,
those crook-backed men
who've thumbed through voice
prints of every silence
we ever touched,
my cry laid bare
so cleanly they jeered,
'Do you always fuck in B-flat?'
and wished me
shchaslivo, good luck,
with a slab of milk-white pig fat,
their *salo* snack
on sour bread
for breakfast."

On the Dong Beat

In that cold country
Hogg trying to be cool
sang a song at the dong
beat of the bell, on the 1-3:

...got a toothpick in my hand,
dig a ten foot ditch,
running through the jungle
fighting lions with a switch

'cause you know I love you baby
yes you know I love you baby
Mona Lisa was a man.

After staring at him a long time she said:
"Is that why children
always paint her
with a moustache?"

There Is No Lenin But Lenin

A craniologist spooned out Lenin's brain and slid it radiant as sunlit suet on to a steel tray, eager to locate the electrical pulse of the revolution in a mathematical equivalent. By building a ladder of electrodes (that looked like mountain florets, he thought) across Lenin's brain, he isolated a cardinal number (20 x each 5 year plan), defined as One, followed by a googol of zeros 000000000000000000000000000000000 representing the population in an historical process of equalization. No possible maximum number could exist in this continuum since the minimum, or single proletarian, could always be added to finite numbers, 3=2+1, 4=3+1, 5=4+1 (Lenin called the obverse "the inevitable increment of victims," whose numbers also progressively increase), achieving an infinity that is actual, a dialectic made finite, filleted from Lenin's brain by the craniologist who took a specimen wafer on his tongue — "to taste the visionary light" — an official report said, the wafer becoming cold flame. His throat suffered third-degree burns. He was fed through a tracheotomy tube, wired up to monitoring machines and put on intravenous. In his state he withered away.

Inside Out

Feeling
open and free
she locked
the door
and swallowed
the key.

They went to bed
and
by keeping
score
of each petite
mort

mocked the dead
who
knocked
at
the door
trying
to
get out.

Tomorrow's Man

Smerdikov the shiv flopped
a folded newspaper onto his lap

and out slid a stolen pewter mirror.
"Only blue bloods, no *blatnye*, preened

in this glass, Hogg. It's grift for you, a gift."
He flashed a gold tooth, wore pegged trousers

with a metallic thread in the herringbone:
"Yevtushenko, he shucked

a dozen oysters in a zoot suit at the Astoria hotel.
So I do like the poet did."

Hogg cracked a bottle of Stolichnaya and propped
the mirror on the front page of *Pravda*,

cropping a head-shot of Brezhnev
saluting the Berlin wall.

"You know what this Yevtuschenko read?
His how to say Yes, how to say No poem.

He should wise up in his mind,
he's too much gimme, too much obliged

to all those eels in
double-breasted suits, apparatchiks

lurking in the Lubyanka reeds.
With me it's the *musara*, the police,

in for the *plantchik* plus whatever I nick.
Socialist to a T, I don't believe in private property.

Only knuckleheads don't know
our courts connive in crimes co-opted

by the cops. But you, my sweet *soplyak*..." He hunkered
into Hogg's face, cunning in his yellow eyes,

"You've got a disease, infectious. Like an angel worried
he hasn't earned his scars, you stare every man

in the eye, asking—'Why are only lice
dancing on the ice? Where did everyone go?'

Before you get iced by the icemen,
cop a leper's bell, or better, lie down and park

your wings in the snow." Hogg, cradling the bottle, thought—
Only dogs have yellow eyes.

Smerdikov stroked the bristle of his lean jaw
in the mirror. "This country's history is a breathing

corpse. I'm the left hand in its right pocket.
Watch me pick it clean."

The Dog Days of History

The noseless slut
had a dog,
a dirty dog had she.
She fed it, she fed it,
she fed the horny runt.
It slipped
up her petticoat
to keep her company,
and
wined there
and
dined there, so
deep in the pink, so
deep in the drink it
never did
see the laugh lines
around her cunt.

At Dostoievsky's Grave

Dusk, the hour so poised
that light and dark cast no shadow
on the straw over a fresh grave
in Aleksandr-Nevsky Laura cemetery.
A man with an attaché case locked to his wrist
watched from the gate
as she touched Dostoievsky's teal blue bronze cheek.
Snow petals fell from the trees,
St. Christopher stood in a river
of stone waves, a girl in his arms.
They held each other beside a cast-iron crypt.
"Before he drowned, my father,
trying to console me,
said love is a silent prayer
sung for the living
by the dead."

Shearing

Hogg had been awake all night, unable to sleep, and when he told her that a man has to have sleep she told him about sheep, white and black sheep on either side of the border. She told him how black sheep crossed to be with white sheep and turned white and how white sheep crossed to be with black sheep and turned black. But one day God took away the border, pulling it like a rope through the long grass and all the sheep turned grey as they chased the rope to the end of the world and disappeared into nowhere and that is how God, who has to keep an open eye on things if He is going to be God, stays awake, by counting sheep.

He is still counting sheep because the sheep keep coming.

Hogg Speaks of Simple Mathematics

There were
men and women
on a hill.

There was a loaf,
there was a fish.

It is a bitter pill
but the loaves are gone,
the fishes, too,

and all those fed
are lain down
among the dead.

Of the multitude,
we were two
and
now are one.

What is less
is more,
a plus.

The miracle of
multiplicity
is us.

Hogg Attends a Café Performance
of Apollinaire's *The Poet Assassinated*

…And the crowd cried in the dark:
    "Who are you? Who are you?"
        (spotlight)
The poet turned east on his heel.
"I am Viperdoc, expunged apple of Eve's throat,
    unlacing Adam's shoes."
The crowd laughed at this rib-tickler.
        (spotlight)
A man in the first row smacked Viperdoc with a blackjack.
    Blood.
A thrown stone that had eyes in the back of its head broke
    his nose.
    Blood.
A fishmonger elbowed her way through the crowd.
"Haw. You. I know you, you cop, you poet, you
    lying pig."
She cold-cocked Viperdoc and spat.
"Look," he said, his hair standing on end,
    "a miracle, it's my brainstorm."
        (pinpoint lights)
She burst his eye with the point of her umbrella.
He fell among women, who beat him. They popped
    his other eye.
"I confess my consolation resides in the raw elegance of
    words…"
"Shut up you bastard. Step aside ladies." A man wagging a
butcherknife jammed it down Viperdoc's throat. Knives. And
knives. In the back, in the heart. Soon, there was only a corpse,
    like a barbed sea-urchin.
        (lights out)

The Leningrad Evening News

Was it a rat? Or the squeal
of a misshapen shoe?
They held close to the stairwell's
stained walls,
the yellow terrazzo seeping cold sweat.
From her corridor on the fourth floor
they heard muffled steps below,
closed the door,
took off their clothes and stood
in the window staring at drifting
ice going out to sea
and what seemed to be a small grey dove,
one wing frozen to the ice.
They touched, kissed, and prayer
shuttled from hand to mouth.
"It's too bad in the morning we can't disappear like stars."
There was a knock
on the door, then the lock
unlatched. A lean man
in a longshoreman's leather coat,
eyes embedded in ash,
told them they had to go. She let him see her breasts
as she bent to slip on her shoes.
"Slut," he said. She brushed his hand.
"You could pass for my father,
except you must shave your moustache."
On the dimly lit landing an old woman,
the glint of ice in her eyes,

soggy bread and six swampy
potatoes in her lap,
sat waiting and watching,
wrapped in newspapers.
"There's a constant chill," she said.
"Constant. But it's old women like me
who keep the news warm."

Her Potato Song

One potato, two potato,
three potato, four,

mother's in her cradle,
her cradle

is her grave,
father's unstable

walking
on a wave,

for every lie
I've told you,

I'm going to tell
you more,

one potato, two potato,
who is keeping score?

Escape Route

"Yes, yes, I lied.
My father didn't drown,
he lay in bed steeped in pain,
his dying eye
spun round the room, hit a wall, went blank,
that blankness at the core
of pain where I imagine
the awareness of life being over begins.
I thought about how he created me,
how he'd candled the night
with my mother's burning hair,
but there he was
flat on his back,
betrayed by his body,
by the night bloom in his side,
an orchid of black light
seminated in the bone.
I beat his sharp bones, I beat them and beat them
until a last breath of air escaped.
He was free, so was I."

The Grinder

Under an iron bridge, a scissors
grinder who wore a red woollen cap
slid his whetstone and bell
into a felt sack
and sat down on a small pier,
clearing light snow away with a whisk.
A bait line of hooks hung from his belt.
"Your blessing, little son," he cried. "Your blessing."
Hogg crossed the air.
The grinder stared out to sea
and then pushed a stone off the pier.
It broke through soft ice.
"The sea lives forever, it swallows its own," he said,
"and so does man, too."
He had a simple pole, lead sinkers,
and an old first-aid box
painted white with a red cross.
It was full of bait.
He fastened pork rind
to his hook
and let his line play
into the eye-hole
in the ice.

Then There Were Eleven

His days wore down
like the heel of a shoe,
but still Hogg was unprepared
for the police
who
elbowed him
off
the street,
stood him
on a cold floor
in his bare feet and
told him
to count his toes,
from
one-to-ten
until he got
to
eleven,
and then,
when
he came up short, said:
"Here are your shoes, if they fit,
wear them to the airport."

Bird Song

The dove flew back to Hogg,
a branch in bloom
in its beak,
a black flower plucked
from the hair of Shulamith
who'd gone up in smoke—
"It was a German Jew, 1914,
who invented Zyklone B
to gas French soldiers, and tommies, too;
his wife, also a chemist, ashamed
of the dead flensed to the bone
by trench rats
shot herself in the heart: such is life,
a soul handcuffed
to a stench too human.
Even so,
I still believe a song
sung is stronger than salt,
but I'm a bird
whose gift lies
in coming down to earth.
If you've been given the gate
by ossifying officials
and they're about to
bury the soft
call of her name in the clouds,
then let's be nimble in the knees and be gone."

Smerdikov's Fish Song

Smerdikov told Hogg
that
the line
between
music and noise
is
silence

and
the line
between
mendacity and complicity
lies
in the
story

but
he
also said
even

a
fish
wouldn't get caught
if he
kept
his mouth
shut.

Puppy Love

"I tell you true,
of course I lied. I lie and lie.
Even about lying. It's how
I made love to you,
in love, like a blind
puppy being drowned,
swallowing the dark
as if it were air,
choking on air,
crying
I'm free, see, see,
there's no despair, no prayer,
only you. Yes, you, and no,
I was not afraid, no I'm not,
it's true,
everything else I said to you was a lie."

As Close as They Came

They made love face to face
unafraid of the dark,
and then in the morning
watched a ladybug
ease along
a window pane
suckling
light.
It was as close as they came
to complete silence.

True Love

Sub-zero, white
jade on the window
pane of an Aeroflot transit room
where Hogg waited alone
except for a baggage handler
who sat winding and unwinding
footcloths from his felt boots:
"I did a tenner
in a gulag work gang
on six ounces of bread a day.
I knelt and I prayed, too,
till my brain sang
like a mourning dove
purified
anointing the air
with a cry:
O thou
dark pearl,
I have merged
utterly
in wonder,
dark pearl,
in thee,
thy dolorous name,
my only
Cell."

So It Was Done

It all begins at the end.
We know what love is
when it's over,
the trail of two people
bending into the echo of their own laughter
across a lake fresh with snow.
"And this, this," she cried, looking back,
"is the whiteness of God's mind.
Without us he is nothing.
Nichevo, nichevo."

Canto XXXIV
(fragmento)

    ...sometimes when a mist
is blown down or when night wheels along
this latitude a windmill turns within
eyeshot...

    ...ghosts
are encased like bits of straw in clear ice,
some splayed, some upstanding as poles,
or head over their heels, or head-first,
or gripping their ankles, face down...
    ...in a place
where he'd need to wear all his courage on
his sleeve, chilled to the bone, weak in the knees,
"I am a dead man walking..."

...as the ruler of the doleful city rose
upright in ice...
    ...three faces
in his head, the frontal face colored red.

...a mangled prisoner, in each mouth torn
skin between the teeth...
    ...so he and
his guide kept climbing without pause until they got
to high ground where he caught sight,
through a round hole in the eroded
stone, of a beauty embedded in the sky.
Then they were out and could see stars.

Seven Last Words

In the fluted air under a carousel
of polar light
a chord was played on fretted bone.
Chimes of snow.
A quick fly strutted
on stilts,
beheaded notes
of their cry.
She gave him a weightless kiss
through the waiting-room glass
and said:
"Each night I die
but it is not
goodbye.
Ice is only rain yielding life again."

Hope

Death,
like the night,
only
darkens
the
door
of
day
at dawn
long
enough
to
disappear.

Hogg's Notes

Now we're on my home ground, foreign territory.

Margaret Atwood

Not a Thorn, Not a Tree: This poem contains Hogg's translation of "The Knee" from *Gallows Songs* by the German poet, Christian Morgenstern. Hogg treasured a particular poem in this sequence because it seemed a pure elegiac response to the old Russian saying, "When someone hiccups he's remembering dead men." The poem, a sonnet, was "Fishes' Nightsong":

Air, Air, Air: Feodor Dostoievsky placed Raskolnikov's yellow room in *Crime and Punishment* at 7 Pergevalsky Street, apartments clustered around a dank courtyard where Dostoievsky also lived for a time. One evening at dusk, Hogg stood in this inner court and sang at the top of his voice:

> *When I was in that railroad wreck*
> *Who took the en-gine off my neck?*
> *No-body.*
> *I ain't never done nothing to nobody*
> *And nobody's done nothing for me.*
> *No-body. No, no-body.*

Several residents, none of whom could speak English, came into the yard and insisted on singing along, over and over:

> *No-body,*
> *No-body, No-*
> *body…*

At the Station of the Noseless Slut: The noseless slut was Anna Akhmatova's endearing name for Death.

Ice Fishing: Lubyanka, secret police headquarters and prison in central Moscow. Before the 1917 Revolution, the building housed the Rossiya Insurance Company. Hogg was told that the Company's motto was: *We Are With You To The End.*

He Loved a Floating Apple & **The White Fairy Tale** are Hogg's translation and adaption of the poet, Imants Ziedonis, who wrote in Latvian in the occupied city of Riga.

Stones: When Vladimir Mayakovsky shot himself through the heart in 1930, he left behind a verse that began:

> *And, as they say,*
> *the incident*
> *is closed.*
> *Love's boat is sunk*
> *by the daily splunk.*

In telling Hogg about her father, the woman altered the cliché *intsident ischerpan* (the incident is closed) to *intsident isperchen*, as did Mayakovsky in his suicide note—*isperchen* meaning something like *a biting tang* too hard to swallow.

Himmler's Law: In *Genesis*, chapter 19, Abraham, Lot's uncle, is in the hills watching as "the smoke of the country went up as the smoke of a furnace." His call, "most brightly of all burns the hair," is a line from Paul Celan's long poem, *Deathfugue*. Celan was a Romanian Jew who wrote cryptic, riddling poems under the shadow of death: his parents died in a German extermination camp; he wrote in the language of his enemies, German; he committed suicide by drowning in 1970.

Cold Comfort: *Osobeast* is an officer of the special Branch, representing State Security, usually in a military unit—"the Osóby Otdél."

Promise of Rain: Marina Ivanovna Tsvetayeva is the woman's namesake and bedside poet (1892-1941). She consistently cut against the grain, praising the White Army while writing in Red Moscow. Pasternak said she "was a woman with an active masculine spirit, determined, warring, indomitable...she strove avidly, recklessly, almost rapaciously for clarity and finality." She lived in Paris from 1922 to 1939; while there, she said she "would like to be buried in the flagellants' graveyard in Tarusa (her father's birthplace) in one of those graves with a silver dove on it." Two years after her return to the Soviet Union she committed suicide by hanging.

WORK MAKES FREE is *ARBEIT MACHT FREI,* cast in iron in the arch over the entrance at Auschwitz.

Osip Mandelstam Moves His Lips: A poet who "made himself an expert in farewells." He died "at the age of 47 in a concentration camp, a starving, insane prisoner who, imagining that he was being systematically poisoned, was reduced to hunting for scraps of food in garbage dumps." His arrest came after Lev Gumilyov, the son of Anna Akhmatova, made the mistake of reading a Mandelstam poem, a lampoon of Stalin, to friends. An informer alerted police to the caricature:

> *turns to the Kremlin mountaineer,*
> *the ten thick worms his fingers,*
> *his words like measures of weight,*
> *the huge laughing cockroaches on his top lip.*

Gumilyov was arrested just before the War, put in prison, released to fight on the eastern front, and after the fighting, sent back to the Gulag to disappear. Mandelstam's wife, Nadezhda, wrote: "A certain friend of mine from across the ocean once said to me: 'Any poet of ours would be glad to change places with any one of yours.' 'With all the consequences?' I asked. 'Yes,' he replied. 'Poetry's a serious business with you.' In my opinion he underestimated the consequences. In the 'breathing space,' years during which this conversation took place, even Akhmatova had begun to forget about consequences, and what they are really like. At this period, astonished at how people abroad—in particular, Russian émigrés—utterly misunderstand our life, Akhmatova often repeated a phrase which infuriated me: 'They are envious of our suffering.' Such failure to understand has nothing to do with envy—it comes from the impossibility of imagining our experience and also from the deluge of lies by which reality has been twisted out of all recognition. To this one must also add complete unwillingness to think things out. I find it impossible to credit such lazy and indifferent people with the power to feel ordinary sympathy or even a drop of pity, never mind envy. They just didn't give a damn and looked the other way. But the main thing is that there was nothing to envy. There was absolutely nothing at all uplifting about our suffering. It is pointless to look for some redeeming feature; there was nothing to it except animal fear and pain. I do not envy a dog that has been run over by a truck or a cat thrown from the tenth floor of a building by a hooligan. I do not envy people, like myself, who suspected a traitor, provocateur, or informer in everyone and did not dare utter their thoughts even to themselves for fear of shouting them out in their sleep and giving themselves away to the neighbours on the other side of the thin walls that divide our apartments. There was, I can tell you, nothing to envy."

x, **the Starting Number:** The mathematical formula reflects an assertion made in "Fit The Fifth: The Beaver's Lesson" from Lewis Carroll's *Snark*. The Beaver, trying to determine if he has actually heard the three cries of the Jubjub bird, proposes a fact-finding formula:

> *Taking Three as the subject to reason about—*
> *A convenient number to state—*
> *We add Seven, and Ten, and then multiply out*
> *By One Thousand diminished by Eight.*
>
> *The result we proceed to divide, as you see,*
> *By Nine Hundred and Ninety and Two:*
> *Then subtract Seventeen, and the answer must be*
> *Exactly and perfectly true.*

Working out this formula allows The Beaver to state with conviction that a Jubjub, the bird that holds Hogg in its beak, not only exists, but

> *As to temper the Jubjub's a desperate bird,*
> *Since it lives in perpetual passion.*

Two passionate Soviet scientists of a literary bent, Stanislav Rodionov and Gersh Budker, sat down one night in 1960 in Akademgorodok to refine what they called their revolutionary "Alice in Wonderland" machine. They were working out problems in particle physics, a proton-antiproton project set up to probe the basic properties of matter. To relieve the intellectual tension, Rodionov read aloud for an hour from Agatha Christie's *Cards on the Table*—a story involving the criminal permutations and combinations of eight bridge players and four murderers. Then, the two men created a colliding beam machine that sent two beams of electrons and positrons (the electron's antimatter counterpart) at nearly the speed of light to meet head on like fields of race horses running around a track in counter rotating directions. The resulting collisions allowed them, for the first time, to enter into the realm of antimatter, a looking-glass world. The *Antiworlds* poet, Voznesensky wrote:

> ...*let the antiworlds be praised,*
> *the fantastic in our humdrum days!*
> *Who would be sane if it weren't for the mad...*
> *The world of science is dead right.*
> *Like a radio my cat lies*
> *Tuned in to the world through her green eyes.*

Hogg Attends a Performance of *The Exile* at Café Tristan Bernard: Tristan Bernard died at the age of eighty-one in 1947. He wrote forty plays and fifty novels, and was known as the "French Mark Twain." He was best known for *The Little Café*, the play that launched Maurice Chevalier on his movie career, and *As It Is Spoken*, which was a standard at the Comédie Française. *The Exile*, written in 1932, as Stalin solidified his power, is the shortest play— other than Beckett's *Breath*—ever staged.

Hogg Meets Isaac Babel: The words spoken by the old man are—in response to the great Tolstoiyan question—from a story by Isaac Babel set in the Peski district of St. Petersburg one year before the Revolution. It is called "Guy de Maupassant." It is a story about translation. Hogg liked to think of Babel's narrator, decades after Lenin, after Stalin, meeting himself and his woman, Marina—who was a translator—on a Leningrad street. Babel was arrested during the Stalin purges in the late 1930s and died in 1941 in a concentration camp.

The Old Believer: Old Believers, a sect founded in the second half of the seventeenth century. There is a Mussorgsky opera, *Khovanshchina*, about the conflict between Peter the Great and the boyars, the religious struggle between the Old Believers and New Believers. Hogg was told that the religious dispute was over the number of fingers to be used in making the sign of the cross. In the 1920s and 1930s the religious education of your own children was a political crime under Article 58-10 of the Code. The poet Tanya Khodkevich got ten years for writing:

> *You can pray freely*
> *but only if God alone can hear.*

Little Father was a name of awe and affection for Stalin among ordinary Soviet citizens. But many party members and sophisticated intellectuals who aspired to build a new society were also abject in their willingness to denounce, their willingness to cry *slovo i dielo*. Anyone could denounce anyone to the NKVD, and even a member of the Politburo and the general secretary of the Comintern, Nikolai Bukharin, after his expulsion from the Party and before his execution in 1938, wrote a final self-abasing letter to Stalin: "...it would be petty for me to place the question of my own person *on a par* with the *universal-historical* tasks resting on your shoulders...My heart boils over when I think that...in your heart of hearts you yourself think that I am really guilty of all these horrors...My head is giddy with confusion, and I feel like yelling at the top of my voice...I ask you for forgiveness, though I have already been punished to such an extent that everything has grown dim around me."

The *Streltsi*, meaning *shooters*, were Russia's first permanent infantry force of the sixteenth and seventeenth centuries. Under Peter the Great these household troops became a xenophobic fundamentalist force, glorifying the Old Believers, rioting against Peter's 'westernizing' reforms. Peter crushed them in 1698. Two thousand were put to death. They were quartered and hung from the Kremlin's towers.

Great Peter: Peter the Great was Czar from 1682 to 1725. He opened Russia to the West by building St. Petersburg out of the swamps found along the banks of the Neva. The city was officially renamed Petrograd, 1914-1924, and then Leningrad, and then St. Petersburg again in 1989, after *perestroika* and the hauling down of the Berlin Wall. The Winter Palace, erected between 1754 and 1762, was stormed in 1917, signalling the October Revolution.

Vladimir Bukovsky, the Soviet dissident (with whom Hogg marched in protest against the Helsinki Accords in the Finnish capital in 1985) asked, "Why are Leningraders such plotters? Some heap the blame on Peter the Great: he was the villain of the piece. Raped poor old elemental Russia, who gave birth to a bastard that has plagued us ever since.

"At least one of his crimes is self-evident—he up and built Saint Petersburg, a city of plotters. He built it with malice aforethought, probably when he was hung over, which is why the city is permanently enveloped in fog, which poisons everyone with a passion for plotting. The Petersburgers lurk in their homes, storing up their secret thoughts, and perceive every acquaintanceship as a clandestine link.

"Arriving in Leningrad from the Moscow station one early spring morning, I wandered down its dazzling, deserted avenues and admired the sumptuous architecture. Every building is an aristocrat, looking condescendingly down its nose at you. But all you need to do is penetrate behind the façades, into the maze of damp, gloomy, well-like courtyards, and it hits you at once— *this* is its home, *this* is the source of that Leningrad underground psychology. You can talk to Leningraders only one at a time, in a whisper, and they never introduce you to anyone else: 'Oh dear no, I live alone—I don't have any friends.'

"Gaffer, one of my former cellmates in the psychiatric hospital, seemed created to arouse the immediate suspicions of the Soviet man in the street—he looked too much like a foreign spy in a Soviet film. Short, fat, and bald, peering out watchfully through thick-lensed specs, he was the very image of an agent of world imperialism. Even schoolchildren used to stop in the street and stare after him—should we call a policeman? Making my way to his home by way of Leningrad's backyards and backstairs, I invariably intercepted wary looks from his neighbours: 'Another visitor for our spy.' He was an arch conspirator, had already done three spells in the mental hospital, and was so inured to leading a double life that by now he virtually plotted with himself. Each time he was released he was restored to membership in the Party and got himself a job in the ideological sector— writing articles for the Party press or working as an instructor. In short, he 'wormed his way into a position of trust' and 'camouflaged himself.' One day in Moscow he went with me to visit a typical rowdy Moscow apartment and was overcome with indescribable horror. 'This is a trap,' he hissed in my ear, 'we've all been had. We must leave at once.' He had a regular plot going. Friends were hard to find in the Leningrad fogs, but conspirators were ten a penny. Looking twenty years younger, he scurried about Leningrad, busy with his conspiratorial meetings, secret rendezvous, and negotiations...

"It always seems so tempting, so simple and so justified—to answer the Red Terror with the White Terror, the White with the Red. Look, they are torturing us, they are beasts, not human beings! Why can't we torture them? Watch, they are openly robbing us—what are we waiting for? Their impunity only encourages them. And if the state is exercising coercion anyway, why not use coercion in the name of justice, and in the name of their salvation too?

"But I was born in a year when the whole of mankind, whether it wished to or not, was at loggerheads over the colour of its concentration camps—brown or red. One thing was clear to me: man's liberation couldn't come from outside. It had to come from within, and until the majority of us had freed ourselves of the psychology of the underground, of the rage for justice, our descendants were doomed to go on arguing in their kitchen: 'When did it all begin?' Like ants at the bottom of a mug."

Khishchuk and Ugolov: 1984: The Ukrainian name, "Khishchuk," has its root in the word for "vengeance." "Ugolovniki" are habitual criminals.

Champagne: ANC, the African National Congress. The Congress and the South African Communist Party received not only substantial funds from the Soviets—beyond even the paranoid nightmares of BOSS (the South African security service)—but arms, along with communications equipment. The ANC as we know it could not have existed without this support. ANC leaders, now that there have been free elections in South Africa, refer to the period of Soviet support as "assistance in the most difficult years." Hogg, during these years, spent time in South Africa, was arrested by BOSS, and taken to prison.

Rasputin: The man who watched the *starets* (the holy man) whip Olga Lokhtina as she held on to his prick crying, "You are God," was G. Fillippov, Rasputin's publisher.

What Voznesensky Whispered to Hogg: In 1979, after Andrei Voznesensky and other members of the Writers' Union were unable to get official approval for publication of an anthology, a quatrain by Voznesensky appeared in *Metropol*, privately printed (this is Hogg's elaboration on his lines). Voznesensky once wrote: "The poet is two people. One is an insignificant person, leading the most insignificant of lives. But behind him, like an echo, is the other person who writes poetry. Sometimes the two coexist. Sometimes they collide; this is why certain poets have had tragic ends. Often the real man has no idea what path or what action the other will take. That other man is the prophet who is in every poet…"

WANTED: A POPOV MACHINE: In the 1950s, Oleg Konstantinovich Popov, a clown and tightrope walker, appeared as an apprentice to the great Karandash of the Moscow circus. His act incorporated skills as an animal trainer and juggler. In the late 50s and 60s, as he travelled the western world he was known as the "Sunshine Clown." His intention was to "create joy, not laughter for its own sake."

Sky Queen: Potemkin is a reference to the warship *Potemkin*, notorious because the crew mutinied in 1905, only to be cruelly suppressed by the tsarist police. The mutiny was made famous by Sergei Eisenstein's film, *Battleship Potemkin* (1925). Count Potemkin was a lover and adviser to the Empress, Catherine the Great. Though acutely aware of all the ideas loose in revolutionary France, and wary of those ideas, she was wilfully out of touch with the condition of the millions of serfs in bondage in Russia. (As a precursor to Herbert Hoover, with his election slogan, "A chicken in every pot", she said: "Every peasant has his turkey in the pot every Sunday.") To sustain her sense of opulent well-being, security and isolation, Potemkin erected "cardboard" villages to line Catherine's route on her grand expedition down the Dnieper to visit the Crimea. She was taken in by these Potemkin villages and she was well pleased (as members of the Red Cross were pleased in 1944 to find "carefree, well-fed Jews" in the "cardboard" town of Terezin in Czechoslovakia, outside Terezin camp, transit prison to Auschwitz). To increase his own sense of well-being with music around his palace, in the early 1770s Potemkin paid 40,000 rubles to Field Marshal Razumovskii for a 50-piece orchestra made up of slave serfs. No matter. He fell into deep gloom.

Walter Benjamin wrote: "It is related that Potemkin suffered from states of depression which recurred more or less regularly. At such times no one was allowed to go near him, and access to his room was strictly forbidden. This malady was never mentioned at court, and in particular it was known that any allusion to it incurred the disfavour of Empress Catherine. One of the Chancellor's depressions lasted for an extraordinary length of time and brought about serious difficulties; in the offices, documents piled up that required Potemkin's signature, and the Empress pressed for their completion. The high officials were at their wits' end. One day an unimportant little clerk named Shuvalkin happened to enter the anteroom of the Chancellor's palace and found the councillors of state assembled there, moaning and groaning as usual. 'What is the matter, Your Excellencies?' asked the obliging Shuvalkin. They explained things to him and regretted that they could not use his services. 'If that's all it is,' said Shuvalkin, 'I beg you to let me have those papers.' Having nothing to lose, the councillors of state let themselves be persuaded to do so, and with the sheaf of documents under his arm, Shuvalkin set out, through galleries and corridors, for Potemkin's bedroom. Without stopping or bothering to knock, he turned the doorhandle; the room was not locked. In semi-darkness Potemkin was sitting on his bed in a threadbare nightshirt, biting his nails. Shuvalkin stepped up to the writing desk, dipped a pen in ink, and without saying a word pressed it into Potemkin's hand while putting one of the documents on his knees. Potemkin gave the intruder a vacant stare; then, as though in his sleep, he started to sign—first one paper, then a second, finally all of them. When the last signature had been affixed, Shuvalkin took the papers under his arm and left the room without further ado, just as he had entered it. Waving the papers triumphantly, he stepped into the anteroom. The councillors of state rushed toward him and tore the documents out of his hands. Breathlessly they bent over them. No one spoke a word; the whole group seemed paralyzed. Again Shuvalkin came closer and solicitously asked why the gentlemen seemed so upset. At that point he noticed the signatures. One document after another was signed Shuvalkin... Shuvalkin...Shuvalkin.

"This story is like a herald racing two hundred years ahead of Kafka's work. The enigma which beclouds it is Kafka's enigma. The world of offices and registries, of musty, shabby, dark rooms, is Kafka's world. The obliging Shuvalkin, who makes light of everything and is finally left empty-handed, is Kafka's K. Potemkin, who vegetates, somnolent and unkempt, in a remote, inaccessible room, is an ancestor of those holders of power in Kafka's works who live in the attics as judges or in the castle as secretaries; no matter how highly placed they may be, they are always fallen or falling men, although even the lowest and seediest of them, the doorkeepers and the decrepit officials, may abruptly and strikingly appear in the fullness of their power...We encounter these holders of power in constant, slow movement, rising or falling. But they are at their most terrible when they rise from the deepest decay—from the fathers. The son calms his spiritless, senile father whom he has just gently put to bed: 'Don't worry, you are well covered up.' 'No,' cried his father, cutting short the answer, and threw the blanket off with such strength that it unfolded fully as it flew, and he stood up in bed. Only one hand lightly touched the ceiling to steady him. 'You wanted to cover me up, I know, my little scamp, but I'm not all covered up yet. And even if this is all the strength I have left, it's enough for you, too much for you…But thank goodness a father does not need to be taught how to see through his son.'…And he stood up quite unsupported and kicked his legs out. He beamed with insight…. 'So now you know what else there was in the world besides yourself; until now you have known only about yourself! It is true, you were an innocent child, but it is even more true that you have been a devilish person!' As the father throws off the burden of the blanket, he also throws off a cosmic burden. He has to set cosmic ages in motion in order to turn the age-old father-son relationship into a living and consequential thing. But what consequences! He sentences his son to death by drowning. The father is the one who punishes; guilt attracts him as it does the court officials. There is much to indicate that the world of the officials and the world of the fathers are the same. The similarity does not redound to this world's credit; it consists of dullness, decay, and dirt."

Hogg in the Land of H.: In Russia, when ordering cheap vodka, many ask for a "96.6". While he drank, Hogg read Robert Graves: "It seems that in ancient times swine-herds had an altogether different standing from that conveyed in the parable of the Prodigal Son: to be a swine-herd was originally to be a priest in the service of the Death-Goddess." (When Hogg read this to Marina she smiled slyly.) Graves went on to say that the holy tree of Russia, the birch, was a besom for the expulsion of evil spirits. In the alphabet of the trees, B, the birch (*berezha* in Russian), was used as a cipher equivalent of H (the hawthorne: *boyarishnik*). "So it seems that Sunday's original letter was not B, but H (Hogg is in the 'land of H'), of which the Hebrew tree, corresponding with the hawthorne, was the *Sant* or wild acacia, the sort with golden flowers and sharp thorns, better known to readers of the Bible as 'shittim'-wood. It was from its water-proof timber that the arks of the Sun-hero Osiris and his counterpart Noah were built."

A Blown Kiss: Though the allusion to artichokes and love is a part of Russian folk sayings, Hogg first came across the idea in the memoir of an émigré St. Petersburg writer, Nina Berberova.

At the Winter Palace: The Boyars were a privileged order in the Old Russian aristocracy, next in rank to a *knyaz* or prince. They were also members of the Boiarskaia Duma (Council of Boyars) that advised the Tzar, but they were abolished by Peter the Great.

XB is the Russian abbreviation for *Khristos Voskres* (Christ is Risen) and it often appears on decorated Easter Eggs. Also, these letters sometimes appeared overnight in the cities during the Brezh-nev years of great stagnation, painted on walls and sidings by rebellious youths.

A Little Piece of the Night: *Trotskiticha*, Trotskyite. Lev Trotsky (1879-1940) was one of Lenin's associates and the first Soviet Defence Commissar, until 1925. In a struggle with Stalin he was expelled from the Party in 1927 and deported to Turkey in 1929. He was murdered in a town on the Mexican coast by a Soviet agent. Trotskyism came to mean not just criticizing the Stalinist party line, but implication in conspiracies to assassinate the party leadership.

Orlau, a town in East Prussia. In 1914, the year Christian Morgenstern died, Russian troops and cavalry drove the Germans back, declared a victory, and withdrew. Solzhenitsyn wrote: "As for the fighting at Orlau, how could anyone call it a 'victory'? They had suffered two and a half thousand casualties; they had failed to follow up and pursue; and having found the enemy when they didn't expect him, instead of changing their line of advance they had just kept plodding on in the *wrong direction*. And they thought they had won a victory! Who but Russian generals could indulge in self-deluding joy over such a trivial success?"

On Nevsky Prospekt: Nevsky Prospekt is the central avenue in St. Petersburg-Leningrad. *Zeks* is gulag work camp slang derived from *zaklyuchennye*, Russian for "prisoners" and these cons described their terms of imprisonment as "a tenner" (ten years), "a quarter" (twenty-five years). *Gulag*: the soviet penal system under Stalin in the far northeast sub-arctic archipelago, a Russian acronym for Chief Administration of Corrective Labor Camps. The most notorious area was Kolyma, described in *Kolyma Tales* by Varlam Shalamov. Prisoners in Kolyma began to work before daybreak on "land reclamation" in minus 40 degree weather, hacking with pick and shovel to no avail at the permanently frozen tundra. These prisoners quickly became known as "goners."

Hunger: During the 900-day siege of Leningrad by Hitler's armies, from 1941 to 1944, as men, women and children starved and froze to death, citizens refused to cut down the city's ancient trees for firewood. It is also true (**Heartbeat**) that during the terrifying winter of 1941 a metronome was set up to *tock-tock* behind music played on the local radio station in case the music should go dead.

An Evening Drive: A found poem, re-worked from *Into That Darkness* by Gitta Sereny. She reports a conversation with Albert Hartf of the Reich Security Office, who had been sent to Russia in January of 1942.

The Eyes Have It: Smerdikov may have been Marina's cousin through an illegitimacy in the family. The only patronimic like his is Smerdyakov, the suspected murderer who was the illegitimate brother in the Karamazov family. Smerdyakov's mother, Lizaveta Smerdyaschaya, was known as Stinking Lizaveta. Smerdyakov was contrived from her name. Hogg thought Smerdikov might be contrived from Smerdyakov, and if so, he was not only a cousin to Marina but a distant cousin to the Karamazovs.

The Note: Hogg's note, taken from Albert Camus, was attached to the dove's tail in **The White Fairy Tale.** Camus also wrote: "Creation is the great mime…Even men without a gospel have their Mount of Olives…it is not a matter of explaining and solving, but of experiencing and describing…the work of art…marks both the death of an experience and its multiplication." Hogg recalled that Plato, when he first came to Athens, was a mime who had been working his act in the countryside: mime, the pure idea of the Word.

A Cold Child: Troubetzkoy Bastion, where Peter the Great executed his son, where Gorky and Trotsky were held after 1905, was named after Sergei Petrovich Troubetzkoy, 1790-1860. He was one of the Decembrists (a group of Russian officers who took part in an unsuccessful liberal uprising against Nicholas I in December, 1825), and his death sentence was commuted to exile. He was amnestied in 1856. He argued that a nation always throws up an intelligentsia separate from itself (a century later, Voznesensky—narrowing his vision—made the same point about the poet: as a prophet the poet was separated from himself as a citizen).

A Bird Peeped: *Krysha* is money paid for police protection.

How Would You Feel is based on a particular factual moment in Hogg's translation of a lengthy documentary sequence by

Andrei Voznesensky, *Ditch*. Smerdikov the sharpshooter, Valde-miers the appraiser, Pyotr Mikhailovich the driver, and all else are not in Voznesensky's document. *Shapka* is a cap with earflaps, usually made of fur.

The Acrobat: The denunciation *Slovo i dielo* originated as part of the machinery of the law in 1649 under Tsar Alexei Mikhailo-vich, father of Peter the Great. It concerned the crime of lèse-majesté, treason, dealt with by the Secret Tribunal. During the fol-lowing century, it came to mean any criticism whatsoever of the government. All investigations under the charge were secret and arbitrary. Punishments were terrible. A French astronomer, Abbé Jean Chappé d'Auteroche, who led an expedition to Siberia in 1761 to observe the transit of Venus, described the terror it induced: "The apprehension under which the people live in Rus-sia and the absolute silence observed by that nation, particularly on all matters that have any relation to the government or the sov-ereign, are chiefly caused by the freedom which every Russian, without exception, has to cry publicly: *Slovo i dielo*. Thereupon it becomes the duty of everybody present to arrest the person so denounced…" Literally, *slovo i dielo* means *word and deed*.

Peter the Great tried to tamp down the incredible number of accu-sations under this law by proclaiming that not only the accused but the accuser would be put to the rack to see who was telling the truth. Astonishingly, accusations increased. Solzhenitsyn, in his *Gulag Archipelago*, describes with some bewilderment, the fact that citizens—during the great purges of the 1930s—not only accused their neighbours, knowing that this would lead inevit-ably to their own arrest and imprisonment, but the number of accusations rose year by year.

Phoenix: Ivarr the Boneless, an ancient warrior. Lake Ladoga is adjacent to St. Petersburg-Leningrad, whose canals and rivers run out to the White Sea. Lake Ladoga connects the Neva river to the Baltic Sea.

Bruegel's Two Monkeys: This poem by Wislawa Szymborska, rendered by Hogg, was published in Poland in 1957, one year after Soviet troops had massed along the border threatening to invade as they had invaded Budapest in 1956. Hogg has given his woman Szymborska's voice as she sits to write an exam and is asked questions about humanity, questions that arise out of contemplating Bruegel's painting of two chained monkeys sitting in a window; one monkey ironic, the other roused to prompt her with an answer that subverts any optimistic view of history. He rattles his chain.

There Is No Lenin But Lenin: Karl Marx's early book, *The Poverty of Philosophy*, was steeped in the theological world of Proudhon. The "dynamic principle" Marx injected into the progression of history, later adapted by Lenin, was mystical at its root (Mayakovsky envisioned a feast to celebrate the classless society, to be held in a year of endless zeros). In Marx's time in Germany, the mathematician Edward Kastner suggested that larger numbers could never be reached because there *is* no largest number. His fellow mathematician, Georg Cantor, went further, proposing an infinity made up of a continuum of *finite* numbers. This would give an unending immensity to the finite, not unlike the image of God as described by Saint Augustine in *De Civitate Dei*: "Every number is known to Him whose understanding cannot be numbered. Although the infinite series of numbers cannot be numbered, this infinity is not outside His comprehension. It must follow that every infinity is, in a way we cannot express, made finite to God." Lenin's mystical vision of the withering away of the finite state is something Augustine would have understood, even as he disapproved. Or, as an old Jesuit priest once put it to Rolf Hocchuth, the author of *The Deputy*, "What are six million lives in the eye of God?" What else but the Lord God's inevitable increment of victims, in which the infinite is made finite in the faith of an old priest?

Writing of Lenin's autopsy, Health Commissar Semashko noted, "The sclerosis of the blood vessels of Vladimir Ilyich's brain had gone so far that these blood vessels were calcified. When struck with a tweezer they sounded like stone." Lenin's body was mummified and placed in an hermetically sealed glass case in a pyramidal tomb of red-black granite. Soviet leaders often "took counsel" with the "living" Lenin, but sceptics suggested the head was made of sculpted wax, that it was not the body at all. Professor Boris I. Zbarsky, embalming chemist, opened the case before witnesses, turned the head to the left and to the right, and tweaked the nose. It was not wax. It was, the chemist said, "the living dead." In 1962, a poster reproduced in *Pravda* read: "Lenin Lived, Lenin Lives, Lenin Shall Always Live." His brain had been removed, cut up into a thousand slices and stored under sheets of specimen glass in several drawers in the especially created State Institute for the Study of the Brain in

Moscow. It was studied with the hope of determining the nature of his genius.

Lenin, who was bored to the point of sleep by music and could not stand the presence of flowers in a room, had no use for the genius of Mayakovsky (not even his cartoon polemics like "150,000,000," a poem about a giant peasant, a human trojan horse, who wears 150,000,000 heads and wades across the Atlantic to fight hand-to-hand with Woodrow Wilson), but after Mayakovsky who had written:

> let me lead my soul out
> painlessly
> into infinity

committed suicide, losing a private game of Russian roulette, his brain, too, was put in the State Institute. It weighed 1700 grams, 300 more than the average, and was kept in the Institute's Pantheon room, in a drawer next to Lenin's.

Tomorrow's Man: *Pravda* is a newspaper; the word means *truth*. The editors parroted the Party line, falsifying facts.

When he first appeared in *Look* magazine, it was Yevtushenko's poem "The City of Yes and the City of No" that was translated. The *blatnye* were underworld thieves whose motto was: "You today, me tomorrow." *Soplyak* is the affectionate but slightly contemptuous equivalent of "wimp" or "dickhead." *Musara* technically means "garbage" but is street slang for "pigs"—the cops. *Plantchik* is marijuana. Prisoners sang:

> plantchik plantchik, god's good grass,
> pleasure the pickpockets, you bet your ass.

At Dostoievsky's Grave: The Aleksandr-Nevsky Laura cemetery is in St. Petersburg-Leningrad. Dostoievsky is buried there beneath his bronze bust. Smerdikov, who happened by, made a snowball and threw it at Dostoievsky's head, crying, "Poets, poets, they're all punks. Give me a poem about great composers." Hogg, in the manner of Yevtushenko (*estradnaya*), declaimed:

> There was a man from Vladivostok,
> who tied harpsichord strings to his cock.
> When he had an erection

he played a selection
from Johann Sebastian Bach.

Hogg Attends a Café Performance of Apollinaire's *The Poet Assassinated:* Apollinaire's lengthy prose poem published in 1916 tells the story of the poet Croniamantal who is reputed to have been born in one of one hundred and twenty-three towns in seven countries in four continents. When he died in Marseilles, the death certificate written by Doctor Ratiboul noted—in the same opinion that had been attached to the dead Napoleon—*partes viriles exiguitatis insignis, sicut pueri.* Peoples who read from right to left modified the name Croniamantel to Latnamainorc, but the Turks call him Pata, the Scandinavians call him *quonlum* (meaning *because*) and the Russians call him Viperdoc (meaning *born of a fart*). Hogg was witness to a performance of the assassination and he loosely approximated a small section of the text.

Bird Song: In *The Song of Songs*, the woman is comely and she is black. Her name is Shulamith. In alchemical texts she is the *anima mundi* in the dark embrace of *physis* and her blackness is attributed to the original sin of Eve. In response to the cry, "Return, return, O Shulamite," she appears in Paul Celan's *Deathfugue* as one of the doomed women of Europe (the other is Margareta of Goethe's *Faust*). She goes up in smoke:

> *your golden hair, Margareta,*
> *your ashen hair, Shulamith.*

In the crematorium at Dachau, Hogg had chanted to himself the last verse of the Walrus and Carpenter's song:

> *"O Oysters," said the Carpenter,*
> *"You've had a pleasant run!*
> *Shall we be trotting home again?"*
> *But answer came there none—*
> *And this was scarcely odd, because*
> *They'd eaten every one.*

The inventor of Zyklone B was the Jewish chemist Fritz Haber, born in 1868 in Prussia. In 1911, he was appointed Director of the Kaiser Wilhelm Institute in Berlin and with the outbreak of WWI, as the embodiment of Prussian pride—unquestioning and uncritically accepting the State's wisdom—he became responsible for the development of chemical warfare. He directed the first gas attacks against the Allied troops, organizing and directing the German release of chlorine gas at Ypres, France, on April 22nd, 1915. Somewhere between 5,000-15,000 Allied troops were wounded or killed on that day alone. In 1918, he was awarded the Nobel Prize for his discovery of ammonia synthesis, a process fundamental to explosives. When Hitler became Chancellor and Jewish academics were purged, though his life was not actually threatened because of his distinguished service to the war effort, Haber emigrated, dying suddenly in Switzerland in 1935.

True Love: In his *Gulag Archipelago*, Solzhenitsyn wrote: "A cell and love in the same breath? Ah, well, probably it has to do with Leningrad during the blockade—and you were imprisoned in the Big House... The cells were left unheated, but after all, there were water pipes in the cells that worked and a toilet, and where else in Leningrad could you find that? ... You sit down and half-close your eyes and try to remember them all. How many different cells you were imprisoned in during your term! It is difficult even to count them. And in each one there were people. There might be two people in one, 150 in another. You were imprisoned for five minutes in one and all summer long in another. But in every case, out of all the cells you've been in, your first cell is a very special one, the place where you first encountered others like yourself, doomed to the same fate. All your life you will remember it with an emotion that you otherwise experience only in remembering your first love."

Mayakovsky also had his cell. He "learned about love in Butyrki," a Moscow prison:

> *I*
> *fell in love*
> *with the keyhole of Cell 103.*
> *Staring at the daily sun,*
> *people ask:*
> *"How much do they cost, these little sunbeams?"*
> *But I*
> *for a yellow patch*
> *of light jumping on the wall*
> *would then have given everything in the world.*

So It Was Done: *Nichevo* is Russian for "nothing." On the heels of the 1917 Revolution, futurist and nihilist poets were known as the Nichevoki, who, "after seeing electricity, lost interest in nature…" One of their members, Daniel Harms, was killed for "nothing" by the security police, arrested because he wore a floppy hat and walked with a limp. The Nichevoki said that they had "shaken syntax loose," and revelled in "images of nonsense, ugliness, violence and coarseness," and sought either the "shaggy dog" story or silence, the silence of Vasilisk Gnedov's "Poem of the End" which contemporaries said he recited by standing in tense silence for a minute, or by making a gesture resembling a cross. The poem, translated by Hogg, was a blank page, with no sign of a hiccup:

ACKNOWLEDGEMENT

Thanks to my night riders,
Seán Virgo and David Sobelman

Books *by* Barry Callaghan

⚘ FICTION ⚘

The Black Queen Stories

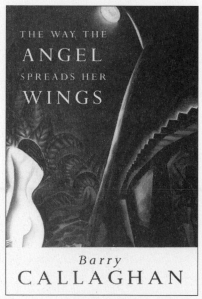

The Way the Angel Spreads Her Wings

When Things Get Worst

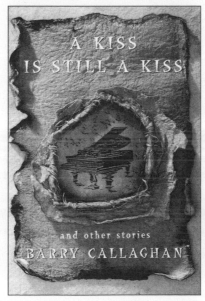

A Kiss Is Still A Kiss: Stories

Hogg, the Poems and Drawings

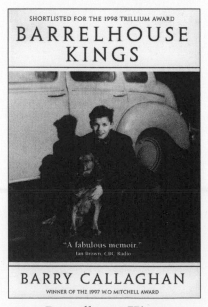

Barrelhouse Kings

❦ TRANSLATIONS ❦
by
BARRY CALLAGHAN

Atlante (Robert Marteau: French)

Treatise on White and Tincture (Robert Marteau: French)

Eidolon (Robert Marteau: French)

Interlude (Robert Marteau: French)

Fragile Moments (Jacques Brault: French)

Singing at the Whirlpool (Miodrag Pavlović: Serbian)

A Voice Locked in Stone (Miodrag Pavlović: Serbian)

Wells of Light (Fernand Ouellette: French;
with Ray Ellenwood)

Flowers of Ice (Imants Ziedonis: Latvian)

This book was set using

Palatino, Galliard
and Hoefler Text Ornament fonts